Quick Colorful Quilts
Beginning with Embellishments

Quick Colorful Quilts
Beginning with Embellishments

Edited by

Rosemary Wilkinson

Good Books

Intercourse, PA 17534
800/762-7171
www.GoodBooks.com

International Standard Book Number: 978-1-56148-575-8
Library of Congress Catalog Card Number: 2006035942

Library of Congress Cataloging-in-Publication Data:
Quick colorful quilts beginning with embellishments / edited by Rosemary Wilkinson.
        p. cm.
   Includes index.
   ISBN 978-1-56148-575-8 (alk. paper)
   1. Patchwork--Patterns. 2. Quilting--Patterns. 3. Machine quilting. I. Wilkinson, Rosemary.
   TT835.Q4536 2007
   746.46'041--dc22
                                    2006035942

Copy Editor: Patsy North
Editorial Direction: Rosemary Wilkinson
Design: Frances de Rees
Photographs: Shona Wood
Illustrations: Carrie Hill
Template diagrams: Stephen Dew

Reproduction by Pica Digital PTE Ltd, Singapore
Printed and bound in Malaysia by
Times Offset (M) Sdn Bhd

NOTE
The measurements for each project are given in imperial and metric. Use only one set of measurements – do not interchange them because they are not direct equivalents.

CONTENTS

Materials and Techniques

MATERIALS

Patchwork fabrics

The easiest fabrics to work with for patchwork are closely woven, 100% cotton. They "cling" together, making a stable unit for cutting and stitching; they don't fray too readily and they press well. Quilting shops and suppliers stock a fantastic range in both solid colors and prints, usually in 45 in/115 cm widths, and most of the quilts in this book are based on these cottons.

Backing and binding fabrics

The backing and binding fabrics should be the same type and weight as the fabrics used in the patchwork top. They can be a coordinating

Battings left to right: silk, cotton, 2 oz cream polyester, black cotton, 80%/20% cotton/polyester, wool, grey and white polyester

color or a strong contrast. You could also be adventurous and piece the backing, too, to make a reversible quilt. In either case, the color of the binding needs to work with both the top and the backing fabric designs.

Batting

Various types of batting are available in cotton, polyester, wool, silk or mixed fibers. They can be bought in pre-cut sizes suitable for crib quilts and different sizes of bed quilts or in lengths cut from a bolt. They also come in different weights or "lofts," depending on how padded you want the quilt to be. Lightweight polyester batting is the most commonly used, but some wool or cotton types are more suited to hand quilting. Some battings need to be closely quilted to prevent them from bunching up; others can be quilted up to 8 in/20 cm apart. Follow the manufacturer's instructions if in doubt.

Quantities and fabric preparation

The quantities given at the beginning of each project have been calculated to allow for a bit extra – just in case! A few of the quilts combine cutting down the length of the fabric with cutting across the width. This is to make the most economical use of fabric or to obtain border pieces cut in one piece.

Unless otherwise stated, any 10 in/25 cm requirement is the "long" quarter – the full width of the fabric – and not the "fat" quarter, which is a piece 18 x 22 in/50 x 56 cm.

All fabrics should be washed prior to use in order to wash out any excess dye and to avoid fabrics shrinking at different rates. Before they are completely dry, iron the fabrics and fold them selvage to selvage – as they were originally on the bolt – in preparation for cutting.

BASIC PIECING TECHNIQUES

SEAMS

To stitch accurately, you must be able to use the correct seam allowance without having to mark it on the fabric. To do this, you use the foot or the bed of your sewing machine as a guide. Many machines today have a "¼ in" or "patchwork" foot available as an extra. There are also various generic foot accessories available that will fit most machines. Before you start any piecing, check that you can make this seam allowance accurately.

Checking the machine for the correct seam allowance

Unthread the machine. Place a piece of paper under the presser foot, so that the right-hand edge of the paper aligns with the right-hand edge of the presser foot. Stitch a seam line on the paper. A row of holes will appear. Remove the paper from the machine and measure the distance from the holes to the edge of the paper. If it is not the correct width, i.e. ¼ in/0.75 cm, try one of the following methods to adjust it:

1 If your machine has a number of different needle positions, try moving the needle in the direction required to make the seam allowance accurate. Try the test of stitching a row of holes again.

2 Draw a line on the paper to the correct seam allowance, i.e. ¼ in/0.75 cm from the edge of the paper. Place the paper under the presser foot, aligning the drawn line with the needle. Lower the presser foot to hold the paper securely and, to double-check, lower the needle to ensure that it is directly on top of the drawn line.

Fix a piece of masking tape on the bed of the machine so that the left-hand edge of the tape lines up with the right-hand edge of the paper. This can also be done with magnetic strips available on the market to be used as seam guides. But do take advice on using these if your machine is computerized or electronic.

NOTES

Seams

Unless otherwise stated, the seam allowances are included in the measurements given and are always ¼ in for imperial and 0.75 cm for metric. The metric seam allowance is slightly bigger than the imperial, but it is easy to use in conjunction with the various rotary cutting rulers on the market.

Measurements

The measurements in the quilt instructions are given in both imperial and metric. Use only one set of measurements in any project – do not interchange them, because they are not direct equivalents.

Stitching ¼ in/0.75 cm seams

When stitching pieces together, line up the edge of the fabric with the right-hand edge of the presser foot or with the left-hand edge of the tape or the magnetic strip on the bed of your machine, if you have used this method.

Checking the fabric for the correct seam allowance

As so much of the success of a patchwork depends on accuracy of cutting and seaming, it is worth double-checking on the fabric that you are stitching a ¼ in/0.75 cm seam.

Cut three strips of fabric 1½ in/4 cm wide. Stitch these together along the long edges. Press the seams away from the center strip. Measure the center strip. It should measure exactly 1 in/2.5 cm wide. If not, reposition the needle/tape and try again.

Stitch length

The stitch length used is normally 12 stitches to the inch or 5 to the centimeter. If the pieces being stitched together are to be cross-cut into smaller units, it is advisable to slightly shorten the stitch, which will mean the seam is less likely to unravel. It is also good practice to start each new project with a new needle in a clean machine – free of fluff around the bobbin housing.

CHAIN PIECING

Have all the pairs of patches or strips together ready in a pile. Place the first two patches or strips in the machine, right sides together, and stitch them together. Just before reaching the end, stop stitching and pick up the next two patches or strips. Place them on the bed of the machine, just touching the patches under the needle. Stitch off one set and onto the next. Repeat this process until all the pairs are stitched to create a "chain" of pieced patches (diagram 1). Cut the thread between each unit to separate them. Open out and press the seams according to the project instructions.

diagram 1

PRESSING

Each project will have instructions on the direction in which to press the seam allowances. These have been designed to facilitate easier piecing at junctions and to reduce the bulk so that seam allowances do not lie one on top of the other.

ADDING BORDERS

Most patchwork tops are framed by one or more borders. The simplest way of adding these borders is to add strips first to the top and bottom of the quilt and then to the sides, producing abutted corners.

Adding borders with abutted corners

The measurements for the borders required for each quilt in the book will be given in the instructions. However, it is always wise to measure your own work to determine the actual measurement.

1 Measure the quilt through the center across the width edge to edge. Cut the strips for the top and bottom borders to this length by the width specified for the border.

2 Pin the strips to the quilt by pinning first at each end, then in the middle, then evenly spaced along the edge. By pinning in this manner, it is possible to ensure that the quilt "fits" the border. Stitch the border strips into position on the top and bottom edge of the quilt (diagram 2). Press the seams towards the border.

diagram 2

3 Measure the quilt through the center from top to bottom. Cut the side border strips to this measurement.

4 Pin and stitch the borders to each side of the quilt as before (diagram 3). Press the seams towards the border.

diagram 3

QUILTING

The three layers or "sandwich" of the backing/batting/pieced top are held together by quilting or by tying. The quilting can be done by hand or machine. The tying is done by hand stitching decorative ties at strategic points on the quilt.

Layering/sandwiching

Prior to any quilting, unless you are using a longarm quilting machine, the pieced top must be layered with the batting and the backing. The batting and the backing should be slightly larger than the quilt top – approximately 2 in/5 cm on all sides. There are two different methods for assembling the three layers, depending on whether the quilt has bound edges or not.

Assembling prior to binding

1 Lay out the backing fabric wrong side uppermost. Ensure that it is stretched out and smooth. Secure the edges with masking tape at intervals along the edges to help to hold it in position.

2 Place the batting on top of the backing fabric. If you need to join two pieces of batting first, butt the edges and stitch together by hand using a herringbone stitch (diagram 4).

diagram 4

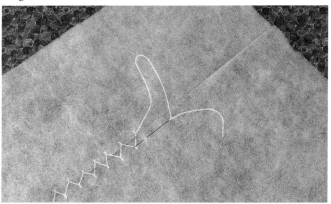

3 Place the pieced top right side up and centered on top of the batting.

Assembling where no binding is used – called "bagging out"

1 Spread out the batting on a flat surface. Smooth out to ensure there are no wrinkles.

2 Place the backing fabric centrally on top of the batting, right side uppermost.

3 Place the pieced top centrally over the backing, wrong side uppermost. Pin with straight pins around the edges to keep them together.

4 Stitch around all four sides with a ¼ in/0.75 cm seam allowance but leave an unstitched opening of about 15–18 in/35–45 cm in one of the sides.

5 Trim the excess batting and backing at the sides and across the corners to reduce bulk, then turn the quilt right side out, so that the batting is in the middle. Slipstitch the opening closed.

6 Smooth out the layers of the quilt and roll and finger-press the edges so that the seam lies along the edge or just underneath.

Basting prior to quilting

If the piece is to be quilted rather than tied, the three layers now need to be held together at regular intervals. This can be done by basting or by using safety pins. For either method, start in the center of the quilt and work out to the edges.

Using a long length of thread, start basting in the center of the quilt top. Pull only half of the thread through as you start stitching. Once you have reached the edge, go back and thread the other end of the thread and baste to the opposite edge. Repeat this process, stitching in a grid of horizontal and vertical lines over the whole quilt top (diagram 5).

diagram 5

Machine quilting

Designs to be used for machine quilting should ideally be those that have one continuous line. The lines can be straight or free-form curves and squiggles. For either type, be sure to keep the density of stitching the same. With either method, continuous lines of stitching will be visible both on the top and on the back of the quilt. It is a quick method but requires careful preparation.

There is a wide variety of tools available designed to help make handling the quilt easier during the machine quilting process. However, the most essential requirement is practice.

It is worth making up a practice sandwich – if possible using the same fabrics and batting as used in the actual quilt – to be sure that you get the effect you want. In any case, plan the quilting design

first, otherwise there is a danger that you will start with quite dense stitching, then tire of the process and begin to space out the lines, producing an uneven pattern.

When starting and stopping the stitching during machine quilting, either reduce the stitch length to zero or stitch several stitches in one spot. If you do not like the build-up of stitches with this method, leave long tails on the thread when you start and stop. Later, pull these threads through to one side of the quilt, knot them, then thread them into a needle. Push the needle into the fabric and into the batting, but not through to the other side of the quilt, and then back out through the fabric again about 1 in/2.5 cm away from where the needle entered the quilt. Cut off the excess thread.

In-the-ditch machine quilting

This is one of the easiest forms of straight line quilting. It involves stitching just beside a seam line on the side without the seam allowances. Some machines require a walking foot to stitch the three layers together. These are used with the feed dogs up and, while in use, the machine controls the direction and stitch length.

Free motion machine quilting

When machine quilting in freehand, a darning foot is used with the feed dogs down, so that you can move the quilt forwards, backwards and sideways. This is easier on some machines than others, but all require a bit of practice. When the needle just "doodles" on the fabric, this is called "vermicelli" quilting.

Hand quilting

The stitch used is a running stitch and the aim is to have the size of the stitches and spaces between them the same. When the quilt is in the hoop, the surface of the quilt should not be taut, as is the case with embroidery. If you place the quilt top with its hoop on a table, you should be able to push the fabric in the center of the hoop with your finger and touch the table beneath. Without this "give," you will not be able to "rock" the needle for the quilting stitch. Do not leave the quilt in a hoop when you are not working on it, as the hoop will distort the fabrics.

1 Thread a needle with an 18 in/45 cm length of quilting thread and knot the end. Push the needle into the fabric and into the batting, but not through to the back, about 1 in/2.5 cm away from where you want to start. Bring the needle up through the fabric at the point where you will begin stitching. Gently pull on the thread to "pop" the knot through into the batting.

2 To make a perfect quilting stitch, the needle needs to enter the fabric perpendicular to the quilt top. Holding the needle between your first finger and thumb, push the needle into the fabric until it hits the thimble on the finger of the hand underneath.

3 The needle can now be held between the thimble on your sewing hand and the thimble on the finger underneath. Release your thumb and first finger hold on the needle. Place your thumb on the quilt top just in front of where the needle will come back up to the top and gently press down on the quilt (diagram 6).

diagram 6

4 At the same time, rock the thread end of the needle down towards the quilt top and push the needle up from underneath so that the point appears on the top of the quilt. You can either pull the needle through now, making only one stitch, or rock the needle up to the vertical again, push the needle through to the back, then rock the needle up to the quilt top, again placing another stitch on the needle. Repeat until you can no longer rock the needle into a completely upright position (diagram 7). Pull the needle through the quilt.

diagram 7

5 When the stitching is complete, tie a knot in the thread close to the quilt surface. Push the needle into the quilt top and the batting next to the knot, but not through to the back of the quilt. Bring the needle up again about 1 in/2.5 cm away and gently tug on the thread to "pop" the knot through the fabric and into the batting. Cut the thread.

BINDING

Once the quilting is completed, the quilt is usually (but not always) finished off with a binding to enclose the raw edges. This binding can be cut on the straight or on the bias. Either way, the binding is usually best done with a double fold. It can be applied in four separate pieces to each of the four sides, or the binding strips can be joined together and stitched to the quilt in one continuous strip with mitered corners. To join straight-cut pieces for a continuous strip, use straight seams; to join bias-cut pieces, use diagonal seams (diagram 8).

diagram 8

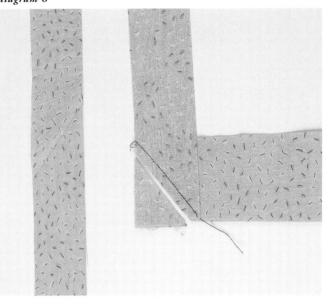

For either method, the width of the bias strips should be cut to the following measurement: finished binding width x four + the seam allowance x two.

For example:

A finished binding width of ½ in would be cut as 2½ in:

(½ in x 4) + (¼ in x 2) = 2½ in

or 1.25 cm would be cut 6.5 cm:

(1.25 cm x 4) + (0.75 cm x 2) = 6.5 cm

Continuous strip binding

1 Fold the binding in half lengthwise with wrong sides together and lightly press.

2 Place the raw edges of the binding to the raw edge of the quilt – somewhere along one side, not at a corner. Commence stitching about 1 in/2.5 cm from the end of the binding and, using the specified seam allowance, stitch the binding to the quilt through all layers of the "sandwich" (diagram 9). Stop ¼ in/0.75 cm from the end. At this point, backstitch to secure, then break off the threads. Remove the quilt from the sewing machine.

diagram 9

3 Place the quilt on a flat surface, with the binding just stitched at the top edge; fold the binding up and away from the quilt to "twelve o'clock," creating a 45° fold at the corner (diagram 10).

diagram 10

4 Fold the binding back down to "six o'clock" aligning the raw edges of the binding to the raw edge of the quilt. The fold created on the binding at the top should be the same distance away from the seam as the width of the finished binding (diagram 11).

diagram 11

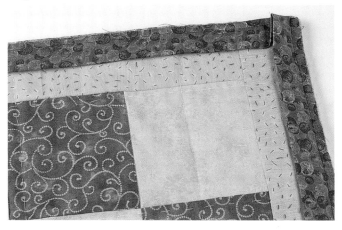

5 Start stitching the binding to the quilt at the same point where the previous stitching stopped. Secure with backstitching, then continue to the next corner. Repeat the process at each corner.

6 Stop about 2 in/5 cm from where you started. Open out the fold on both ends of the binding, then sew the two ends together. Trim away the excess, refold and finish applying the binding to the quilt.

7 Trim the excess batting and backing fabric so that the distance from the stitching line equals or is slightly wider than that of the finished binding. Fold the binding over to the back and hand stitch the folded edge of the binding to the quilt along the row of machine stitching just created. A miter will appear at the corners on the front and on the back of the binding. Slipstitch these in place (diagram 12).

diagram 12

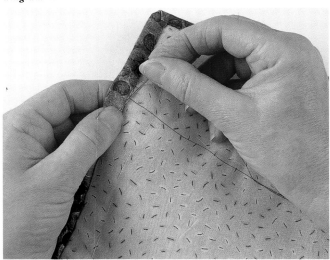

BASIC EMBELLISHMENT TECHNIQUES

Making templates from template plastic

Template plastic can be bought from your local quilt shop in sheets. It is opaque, but strong enough to make accurate, long lasting templates for use in your work. Normally this is used to trace geometric templates off graph paper, which has been marked out; however, it can be used for all shapes and sizes where you need a permanent template to draw around.

1 Lay the template plastic over the shape to be copied.

2 Using a fine permanent marker, trace the shape onto the template plastic.

3 Cut out carefully on the drawn line using a craft knife, with a cutting mat underneath to protect your work surface (diagram 13).

diagram 13

4 Any slight unevenness can be sanded down with an emery board. Template plastic is also useful for making shapes for appliqué and stencils for quilting patterns.

Making prairie points

Prairie points are made from folded squares of fabric and make a delightful edging for a quilt, wallhanging, bag or table runner. You can choose a fabric to match or contrast with your project. A little advance planning has to be done in order to insert them into the edge of the project, but it is well worth the effort.

1 For each prairie point, cut a square – dimensions are given with individual quilt instructions.

2 Fold the first square in half, across the diagonal, wrong sides together, and in half again to form a triangle with four thicknesses of fabric (diagram 14). Press in shape.

diagram 14

3 Measure the length of the edge you are going to add the prairie points to. Work out how many prairie points you will need. The length of the prairie point is measured $1/4$ in/0.75 cm up from the raw edges and they can either be laid with the edges just touching or they can be overlapped. Make up the required number of prairie points.

4 Place the triangles along the edge, with the points facing upwards and aligning raw edges. Pin in place (diagram 15).

diagram 15

5 Place the backing on top, right sides together, pin, then stitch through all layers, leaving a small gap for turning. Turn the work right side out and slipstitch the gap closed. The prairie points will now point downwards and all the raw edges are enclosed (diagram 16).

diagram 16

Foundation piecing

This type of patchwork makes it possible to be very accurate when working on a small scale. The pieces are stitched together using a foundation fabric. You can either purchase the foundation fabric ready-printed with the pattern or you can trace your own design onto calico, freezer paper or lightweight interfacing.

The basic principle is to cover numbered areas of the foundation pattern with fabric on the right side, then stitch them in place from the back, along the drawn lines of the pattern. The seams of the individual pieces are trimmed as you work, then when all the areas are covered, the block can be trimmed down to fit into the specific design. The foundation pattern will allow for $^1/_4$ in/0.75 cm seams all around the edges. If the pattern is marked on a piece of fabric, it is left in place once stitched, but if on paper, this is torn away.

1 Trace and number the sections for the pattern onto the chosen foundation (diagram 17).

diagram 17

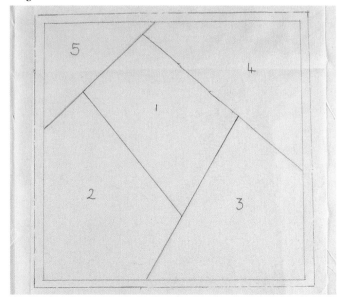

2 Next, choose your fabrics to cover each of the marked pattern areas; they will need to be $^1/_2$ in/1.5 cm bigger all the way around than the shape you want to cover, and they should all have the straight of grain in the same direction.

3 Take the first two fabrics (following the numbers). Turn the foundation so that the marked pattern is on the back. Place fabric number 1, right side up, over shape 1 on the foundation; place shape 2 on top, right side down, pin, then turn the foundation fabric over and stitch on the marked line between shape 1 and 2 (diagram 18).

diagram 18

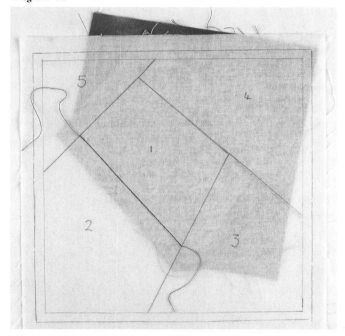

4 Fold the fabrics and the foundation out of the way and trim the seam allowance back to $^1/_4$ in/0.75 cm (diagram 19).

diagram 19

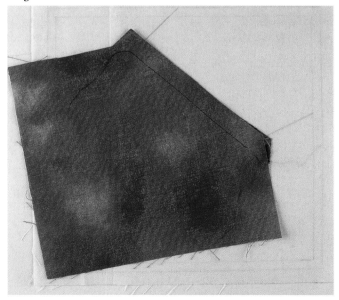

5 Open out fabric 2 and press. Fabrics 1 and 2 should now cover the drawn areas 1 and 2, with a seam allowance overlapping adjacent areas (diagram 20). Repeat with shape 3 and continue until all areas are covered. Trim the block.

diagram 20

Crazy patchwork

Originating from the Victorian era, this type of patchwork ignores the normal rules to combine fabrics of different types and weights, such as velvet, silk and cotton. Here is a method that is a bit out-of-the-ordinary: pieces are tacked to a background fabric, then held in place with hand or machine-embroidered stitches over the seams.

1 Gather together a selection of different fabrics and some matching embroidery threads. Small pieces of fabric are best, and the shapes should be random, not regular.

2 Cut a piece of foundation fabric the size of the finished piece.

3 Starting in the center, lay a piece of fabric right side up onto the foundation fabric. Pin or tack in place. Take the next piece of fabric; lay it down, right side up, next to the first, overlapping very slightly and tack in place. Repeat to add a third piece on another side of the central patch (diagram 21).

diagram 21

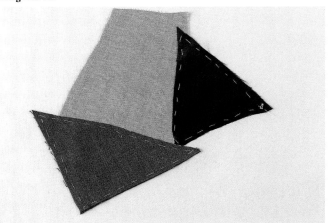

4 When all of the fabric is covered in this way, you can begin stitching over the seams with decorative embroidery threads (diagram 22). Beads and other embellishments, such as small pieces of lace, can also be added. Remove the tacking threads.

diagram 22

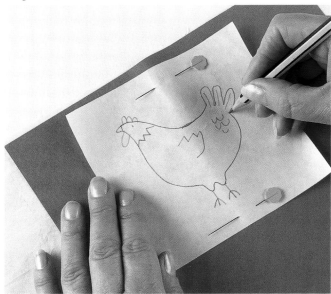

EMBROIDERED EMBELLISHMENTS

Transferring an embroidery design

There may be instances when you want to embellish your work with an embroidery design found in a book or pattern. The easiest way of doing this is to use dressmaker's carbon, which is specially prepared for use on fabric.

1 Trace the design from the original onto plain paper.

2 Place the paper with the dressmaker's carbon underneath onto the right side of your fabric. Pin or tape in place, keeping the work as flat as possible (diagram 23).

diagram 23

3 Draw over the lines of the tracing; you will need to press firmly so that the carbon transfers to the fabric (diagram 24). If in doubt, do a test piece first.

diagram 24

4 You can now use the traced lines to embroider the pattern (diagram 25).

diagram 25

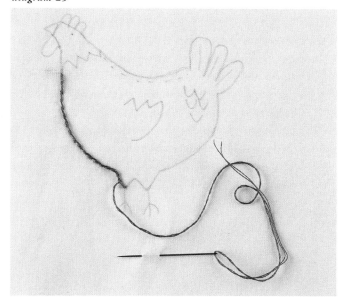

HAND EMBROIDERY

1. Cross stitch

This is a decorative stitch generally used to cover seams on crazy patchwork. It can also be used as an embellishment in the middle of a block. The stitches can be made either singly or in rows.

1 To make a single cross stitch, bring the needle up to the top side beginning in the bottom left corner of the imaginary square where the stitch is to go. Then take it down to the underside in the top right corner to complete the first part of the stitch. Now bring the needle up in the bottom right corner and take back down in the top left-hand corner to complete the cross stitch (diagram 26a).

2 To make a row, working from left to right, bring the needle up to the top side in the bottom left corner of the start of the row and work the first part of the stitch as above. Repeat to work a row of diagonal stitches (diagram 26b), then return along the row from right to left, working each stitch from bottom right to top left to complete the cross stitches (diagram 26c).

diagram 26a   *diagram 26b*   *diagram 26c*

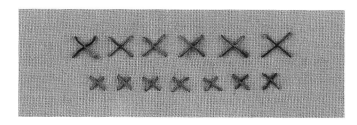

2. Blanket stitch

This is a decorative edging stitch. It is worked from top to bottom or left to right. Bring the needle up to the top side at the edge of the piece to be embroidered. Take it down again below and to the top, then come up again directly opposite this point and level with the start of the stitch, bringing the needle up over the working thread (diagram 27a). Pull gently to make the stitch. Repeat to continue (diagram 27b), anchoring the final loop with a small straight stitch to the back of the fabric.

diagram 27a   *diagram 27b*

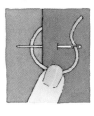

3. Herringbone stitch

This is a decorative stitch generally used to cover seams on crazy patchwork. Working from left to right, bring the needle up to the top side and make a slanting stitch upwards. Take a small horizontal stitch to the left (diagram 28a). Make a slanting stitch downwards and take another horizontal stitch to the left ready to start the next stitch (diagram 28b). Continue in this way to make a row of stitches (diagram 28c). To turn a corner, work the first half of the stitch, turn the work and repeat the horizontal stitch at the top of the row (diagram 28d).

diagram 28a

diagram 28b

diagram 28c

diagram 28d

4. Spider's web roses

This pretty stitch is a type of silk ribbon embroidery. It's made in two parts: the foundation first, then the ribbon weaving. The stages and the finished rose are shown in diagram 29.

diagram 29

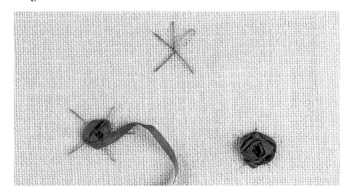

1 Decide on the placement for the rose and mark five spokes of the length you want with a light pencil mark.

2 Thread a large-eyed embroidery needle with thick thread matching the color of the silk ribbon you have chosen. Tie a knot in the end and bring it up from the back through the center of the design. Cover the first spoke by making a large stitch over the marked line. Repeat until all the lines are covered.

3 Thread a length of silk ribbon into the needle (but do not knot it); bring it up in the center of the design, leaving a short tail at the back; now weave the needle in and out of the spokes with slight tension on the silk ribbon, easing the ribbon into place.

4 Repeat until you reach the outer edges of the spokes. The twists and turns of the ribbons will give the appearance of a rose. Take the thread through to the back and neatly fasten off the two ends using a cotton thread.

Decorative stitches by machine

Many sewing machines have built-in or programmable decorative stitches. Amazing results can be achieved when using these stitches in conjunction with the many decorative threads that are available. This book contains projects which enable you to use those stitches in your quilts and you can have fun experimenting with them.

One important thing to remember, if you have a computerized machine, is to make a note of the stitch number, length and width of each decorative stitch before you switch off, as you will lose any record of it once the machine is switched off. Then when you return to the project, you will be able to duplicate the stitches.

1 Referring to your machine manual, select the stitch you require. Your manual will probably tell you which foot, thread and needle is appropriate for the type of fabric you are using.

2 Always do a test piece first. When you are happy with the result, write all the settings on the fabric test piece in pen; you might want to build up a portfolio of these for future reference (diagram 30).

diagram 30

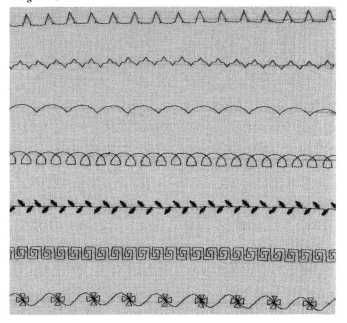

3 Now you are ready to embark on your quilt. Ensure you have a full bobbin and spare needles before you start. These stitches may be used either as an embellishment to the patchwork pieces before the quilt is assembled or as an extra quilting stitch once the batting is in place.

Using decorative thread in the sewing machine

The types of thread that you might consider using in an embellished project are:

Rayon, either solid or variegated, these are shiny and come in many colors (diagram 31).

diagram 31

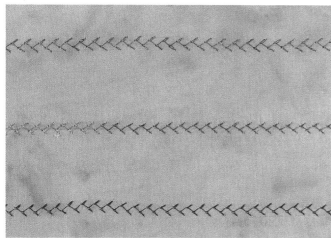

Metallic, the most difficult to use, they are made of a core with metallic thread around, so can be prone to shredding. Normally, these are used for surface decoration, but they can be used for quilting, as can rayon. They can also be used for hand stitching.

Silk, not widely available, but lovely to use.

Cotton quilting threads, these come in so many lovely colors and are good for embellishments.

Your normal sewing thread can also be used quite effectively. Some threads, such as metallic, will need the use of a special needle. They have a groove running down the shaft, to aid the free running of the thread.

Embroidery needles are also available and are finer than normal. These needles are available in a range of sizes.

Note the following points:

1 When using threads you have not used before, it is important to refer to your machine manual for the correct settings.

2 Always prepare a sample first.

3 Very occasionally you may need to alter the tension and/or pressure on your sewing machine. If you do this, make a note of the setting before you change it, then you can put it back afterwards for normal sewing.

ADDED EMBELLISHMENTS

Adding decorative buttons

Decorative buttons are available in many shapes and sizes, and can be used to enhance your quilt. This will normally be done after quilting.

1 First decide where on the quilt you will be stitching the buttons. This can be done by placing them on top of your work until happy with the positioning. Make a note of this to refer to when stitching them onto the quilt.

2 Thread a fairly long needle with a good quality thread and tie a knot in the end of the thread. Bring the needle up through the back of the quilt into the correct position, then gently tug the thread to "bury" the knot in the layers of the quilt. Now thread on the first button, take the needle back down through the free hole in the button and to the back of the quilt (diagram 32).

diagram 32

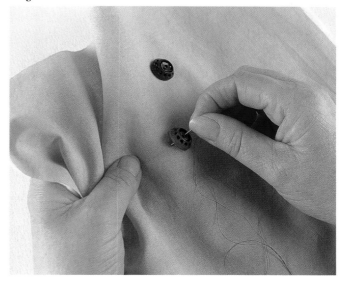

3. Repeat until the button is secure (diagram 33). Secure the ends of the thread as neatly as possible on the back of the work.

diagram 33

Buttons may also be used to tie the layers of a quilt together, a technique known as tie quilting (see page 25).

Adding decorative beads

Beads can be applied to a quilt in much the same way as buttons. Beads are smaller and may need a special beading needle which is very fine and long (to go through the narrow center of the beads). The sparkle they add to a quilt is well worth the amount of work that goes into applying them (diagram 34).

diagram 34

I To add a line of beads, thread the needle with a cotton thread to match the beads and tie a knot in the end. Bring the needle up to the surface from the back of the quilt and add 2 or 3 beads, then take the needle back down into the fabric close to the end of the last bead. Bring it back up on the other side of the last bead and thread through the bead again. Continue in this way until you have the length of beads required, then take the needle to the back of the fabric and secure neatly.

2 To add single accent beads, work as described for buttons above (diagram 35).

diagram 35

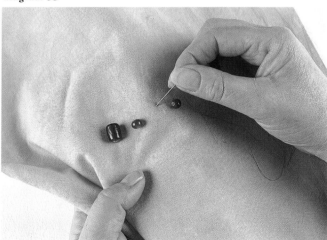

Applying braids, lace and ribbons as embellishments

Braids, lace and ribbons can be particularly good for adding texture and dimension to your work and are available in a huge range of colors and widths. You can also apply handmade cords.

These embellishments can be applied to your work using stitches to hold them in place. This is known as couching.

They can be machine stitched before quilting or hand applied after the quilting stage.

Narrow cords and braids can be machine stitched using a zigzag stitch with the appropriate color thread, which can be matching or contrasting. Normally you would use a zigzag or appliqué sewing machine foot, but if the braid is particularly thick you might need to buy a special foot. Use a fairly open zigzag stitch (not a satin stitch) or any swing needle decorative stitch (diagram 36).

diagram 36

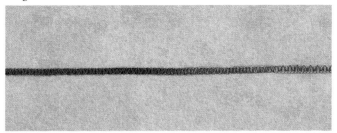

Ribbons can be stitched down either with straight stitches or any of your decorative stitches. Lace may be a little trickier, especially if it is gathered. A little tension may need to be applied to the lace when stitching it down.

It is also important to make sure you have enough braid for the whole project before you begin. Decide on the type of stitch you are going to use, and the best color of thread, then, if possible, do a sample on a test piece of fabric.

I Before stitching any type of braid to your work, lay it on top of the design to decide on the best placement, then when you are happy with the result, pin in place. In some pieces of work you may be able to mark a line to help you when later stitching down.

2 Take your work to the sewing machine, which has already been set up for the correct stitch. Starting slowly, stitch the end of the braid, ribbon or lace to secure, then applying gentle pressure and guiding the braid into place with your hand, stitch it down to your quilt. Do not apply too much pressure or stretch it in any way as this will cause distortion to your quilt (diagram 37).

diagram 37

Appliqué – iron-on method

Appliqué by machine is usually done by the iron-on method. In this method a fusible web is applied to the fabric, which can then be ironed in place onto the quilt. This keeps it in place while stitching. Complicated appliqué designs can easily be built up using this method. Two main stitches are used: satin stitch and blanket stitch.

The fusible web will have a paper-like backing, which you can trace onto. If you trace straight from a book onto the webbing, your pattern will be reversed when you iron it down, so you may wish to trace it out first, reverse it, then draw onto the webbing. Please note: some appliqué patterns have already been reversed for you. Details will be given with the individual projects.

1 Trace the chosen shape onto the smooth side of the fusible webbing. Cut out the shape roughly outside the drawn lines. Take the fabric for the appliqué, and, rough side down, iron the fusible webbing shape onto the wrong side of the fabric. Now cut the shape out accurately following the drawn lines exactly (diagram 38).

diagram 38

2 Next peel off the paper backing, position the shape where you want it on the background fabric, and carefully iron it down. Your appliqué shape will now adhere to the fabric.

3 The appliqué piece is now stitched down around the edges both to add a decorative touch and to ensure that it will not lift off. If you have not done machine appliqué before, I always recommend that you practice first. Set your machine to a satin stitch and do a sample (diagram 39). Every machine varies slightly, so it is important that you make a note of any stitch settings (width and length) that you find works well for you. (You should be able to vary the density of the cover of the satin stitch by altering the stitch length and width.) If, for instance, you practice on calico, you can write the information on the sample of calico.

diagram 39

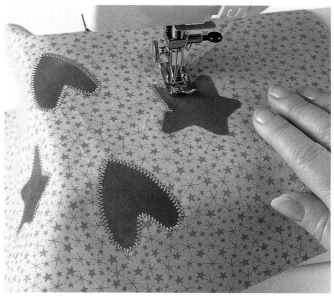

4 It is a good idea to start with the needle down in the fabric, so that you know exactly where you are starting. If the appliqué shape has a gentle curve, then you may be able to maneuvre the machine around the shape as you stitch. The ideal satin stitch or zigzag will cover the edge of the shape, without stitching too much into the background fabric (diagram 40). This takes practice.

diagram 40

5 If you are working with geometric or particularly curvy shapes, you will need to stop at each sharp corner, preferably with the needle down in the work, lift up the presser foot, turn the fabric, put down the presser foot and start stitching again.

NOTE Plan your work so that you change the thread color as little as possible. On a project this could mean doing all of the stitching requiring blue thread first, then the red, and so on.

These hints and tips also apply to the blanket stitch or open zigzag stitch if being used for appliqué.

Broderie perse

This method emerged early last century when fabrics were very expensive and hard to come by. To make the fabric last, or to make its use more economical, motifs, such as large flowers, were cut out of the expensive fabric and stitched onto a background of cheaper fabric. Using this method, cushions, curtains and other soft furnishings could be decorated with a lively pattern. This method can also be used on patchwork using the same technique as for iron-on appliqué above.

1 Identify which motifs are to be cut from the fabric but do not cut them at this stage.

2 Cut out enough fusible webbing to cover these motifs. Iron it onto the wrong side of the fabric, behind the motifs you are going to cut out.

3 Cut out the motifs accurately on the outline of the shape (diagram 41).

diagram 41

4 Peel off the paper backing and iron in place on the background fabric. These can then be decoratively stitched as in the method for iron-on appliqué above (diagram 42).

diagram 42

Making yo-yos

A yo-yo is a simple three-dimensional embellishment made from a gathered circle of fabric. Quite often groups of yo-yos will be used to depict flower heads (diagram 43) or wheels on a quilt.

diagram 43

1 Create a circle template by drawing around a glass, cup or other round object, or use a compass. The diameter of the template should be approximately twice the size of the finished yo-yo.

2 Draw around your template onto the back of the yo-yo fabric (diagram 44).

diagram 44

3 Cut out the circle of fabric.

4 Thread a needle with a length of cotton thread and tie a knot in the end. Turning under a tiny hem of about ¹⁄₈ in/2 mm, work a running stitch all the way around the edge of the circle (diagram 45).

diagram 45

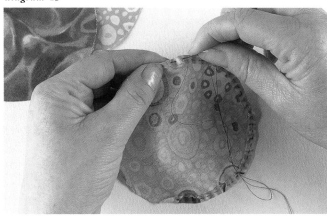

5 Gather up the circle of fabric by gently pulling the thread (diagram 46). Pull up the gathers until only a small circle remains in the center. Secure by stitching a few fastening stitches. Remember the gathered side of the circle is the front – so finish it neatly.

diagram 46

6 Finger-press the yo-yo into shape, so that it forms a regular circle with the gathered side on top (diagram 47). Stitch into place on the patchwork, adding a button in the center if liked.

diagram 47

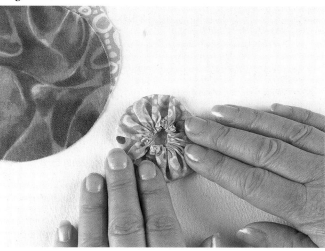

Making folded hexagon flowers

This comes under the larger category of folded patchwork techniques – of which there are many. This one is particularly clever, as it starts as a triangle, and by stitching and manipulation, is transformed into a hexagon. The good thing about folded patchwork techniques is that they end up with all the raw edges enclosed!

1 Using a template, cut out the required number of triangles from fabric – two of differing colors are needed for each flower.

2 Stitch the two triangles together, right sides together, leaving a small gap in one side for turning (diagram 48).

diagram 48

3 Turn, roll the edges between finger and thumb to make a neat seam, then slipstitch the opening closed. Press the work if necessary.

4 Bend all three points in to the center of the triangle, revealing the contrasting color. Secure by stitching, using a matching thread (diagram 49).

diagram 49

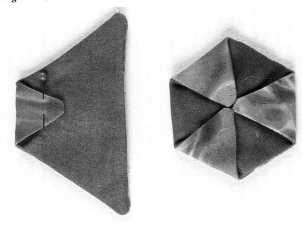

5 You now have a hexagon shape, which when used in a group will resemble a flower head.

DESIGN EMBELLISHMENTS

Printing photographs onto fabric

This technique is fairly new, but has gained in popularity due to the availability of home computers and printers (which just seem to get better all the time). Quilters like to record their memories and this just seems a perfect way of including them in a quilt. Images of any kind can be used, whether it is a child, pet, house, or just a lovely photo. Sheets of specially prepared fabric are available to print onto using your own computer and printer. Alternatively, you can buy a liquid to treat your fabric before printing onto it.

There are several different types of this fabric available, so I would always recommend reading the instructions on the packet before starting. Normally it will consist of a sheet of fabric stuck to a paper backing. Be careful to insert the sheet in the printer correctly. (Refer to the printer manual.)

1 Using either a digital or scanned image, resize the image using a graphics program on your computer. This will ensure that the picture will be the correct size when printed. (There are many graphics programs available, including Paint Shop Pro, a free trial of which can be downloaded, and many others up to Adobe Photoshop, for advanced use.) Please also note that printers will lay down different levels of ink, at different settings. As always, I recommend that you do a test print first onto letter paper to get the alignment right and to check the color balance. By practicing, you will get to know the best settings for your printer.

2 When starting out I also suggest that you take a small sample image and print this several times using all the available options. This can then be retained as a reference (diagram 50).

diagram 50

3 When you are satisfied with all the settings on your printer, insert the fabric as directed and print your chosen image.

Please note that the above refers to ink jet printers. It may be possible to use other types of printers.

Stenciling using freezer paper

Freezer paper is available from all good quilting shops. It is a coated paper, which makes it thick enough for making a stencil. It also has a shiny side which will stick temporarily to the fabric when ironed, keeping it in position while the painting process takes place. The freezer paper is removed later.

It is also possible to apply more than one color to the fabric if required.

This is another situation where it is well worth doing a test sample first, as some paints dry a different color than they appear when first painted. You may also like to practice with the amount of paint you load onto the brush, as getting the right amount is important to the end result.

1 Trace the desired motif onto card stock.

2 Draw around this onto the matte side of the freezer paper (remember this will be reversed when it is ironed down). Cut out the motif carefully and accurately using a sharp pair of scissors (diagram 51).

diagram 51

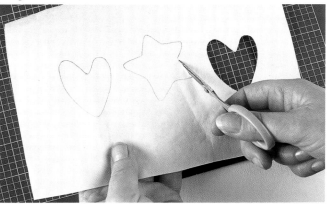

3 Iron the shiny side of the freezer paper down onto the fabric (diagram 52).

diagram 52

4 Using suitable fabric paint, apply the paint sparingly by dabbing with a stencil brush onto the fabric. Leave to dry, then peel off the freezer paper (diagram 53). (It may be possible to use this again.)

diagram 53

5 After drying, iron the fabric according to the manufacturer's instructions, to set the paint.

Flower crushing transfer

With this method the pigment in fresh flowers and leaves is used to color fabric (diagram 54). In the past people used plants such as the skins of onions to dye fabrics: this is just a contemporary version of the same thing.

diagram 54

1 Pick from the garden some deep-colored plants such as pansies and geraniums, preferably fleshy types with open flowers that can be flattened out. Leaves work best if they are quite fleshy, too. Use them right away.

2 Wash and iron the fabric to be used. Cut a piece of freezer paper the same size as the fabric.

3 Protect your work surface with a tea towel. Place the fabric on the towel, right side up. Lay the chosen flower heads and leaves face down on the fabric in the position where you wish the design to appear. (Remove large stalks first so that the flowers lie as flat as possible.) Arrange the flowers in the center first and work your way out. Tape in position with masking tape.

4 Cover the area with the freezer paper, take a hammer and, taking care not to move the flowers, hammer very hard until the pigment from the flowers and leaves is transferred to the fabric (diagram 55). This will take several minutes. To test, carefully lift up the edge of the freezer paper. You will probably notice that the petals have disintegrated or have become transparent. When this happens you will probably have removed all the pigment.

diagram 55

5 Remove the freezer paper and the remains of the leaves, then iron from the wrong side to set the colors.

Dyeing fabric with mottled effect

Dyeing your own fabric adds an individual touch to your quilt. Hand-dyed fabrics can add a representational effect, a mottled blue fabric, for example, could resemble a summer sky. These instructions tell you how to produce a mottled effect, rather than a flat all-over color (diagram 56). Save any old jam jars and also have plastic spoons, rubber gloves and a protective mask on hand before starting. A spare bowl or bucket is also useful.

diagram 56

NOTE Wearing the mask is especially important when handling powdered dyes. Protect your surfaces thoroughly with plastic or newspaper.

1 Wash and prepare the fabric to be dyed. This preparation usually involves soaking the fabric in washing soda first, which will always give a better uptake of the dye. Washing soda (available from supermarkets) is the cheapest way of doing this, or you can buy soda ash from specialist dyeing suppliers. Do not dry the fabric after soaking in washing soda. Some manufacturers may also recommend use of salt as a fixative after dyeing. (Always read instructions before you start.)

2 Mix up each dye you wish to use in a jam jar. To obtain a mottled effect, first prepare the dye bath according to instructions, then roughly fold the fabric and, without disturbing the folds, place in the dye bath. It is best if there is not too much liquid, as this will help you get a mottled effect.

3 For a more controlled effect, the fabric could be knotted, tied with thread, pegged or tied with a pebble inside (tie-dyeing). Whichever method you use you will have a truly unique fabric at the end.

4 Finally when the required time has elapsed (usually at least half an hour), rinse the fabric until the water runs clear. Dry and iron while damp, to eliminate creases.

Dyeing fabric by dripping on several colors of dye

This cold water method involves using more than one color of dye and produces a random effect (diagram 57). A little control can be exercised, for instance if you want one color to be more dominant than another. The basic preparation of the fabric for dyeing is the same as for the mottled dyeing above. You will also need a shallow tray for this method. Have on hand a jam jar for each color of dye you will be using, as well as a separate plastic spoon for each, and avoid contamination between them.

diagram 57

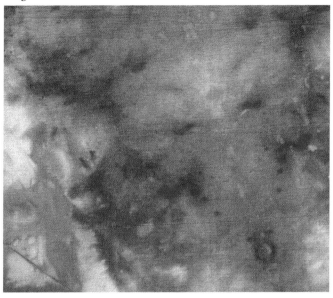

1 Having prepared the fabric, place it wet into the shallow tray.

2 Take the first jam jar and spoon, drip or drizzle dye off the spoon onto the fabric; repeat with all the colors.

3 With experience you will be able to tell whether you have put enough dye onto the fabric. (Ideally there should be none of the original color showing through.) When complete, leave for the required time, then rinse and dry the fabric.

4 An alternative way of doing this would be to fill plastic spray bottles with the dye, so that the different dyes can be sprayed onto the wet fabric. This can also be good if working with children, as it is less messy.

5 Finally when the required time has elapsed (usually at least half an hour), rinse the fabric until the water runs clear. Dry and iron while damp to eliminate creases.

NOTE Keep separate your dyeing utensils and never again use them for food.

Pintucks

Pintucks are a good way of adding a three-dimensional feature to your work. They are not difficult, and for embellishments they provide the quilter with lots of nooks and crannies in which to add embroidery, beads, etc.

1 When you create pintucks your fabric will "shrink" due to the uptake of fabric in the tucks. Make sure you allow plenty of fabric when cutting out to allow for this, usually 10-20% extra.

2 Decide on how many pintucks you would like and how far apart you would like them.

3 Using a patchwork ruler and a pencil (use a silver pencil on dark fabrics), mark vertical lines onto the fabric, evenly spaced, for example 1 in/2.5 cm apart (diagram 58).

diagram 58

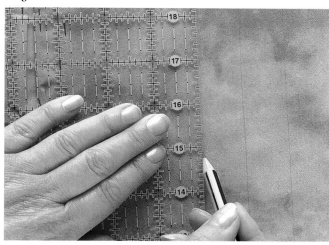

4 Make a small fold on the marked line, taking approximately ¹/₈ in/3 mm of fabric to make each fold or tuck. Pin the fabric vertically to prepare for stitching, so the pins can be removed easily. Repeat for each marked line (diagram 59).

diagram 59

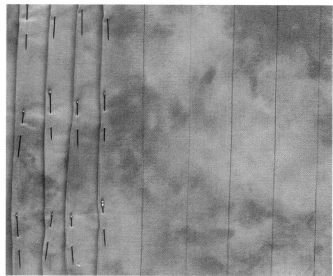

5 Stitch down the lines with a matching thread. Press lightly, or if desired, press to one side (diagram 60).

diagram 60

6 On some sewing machines, tucks can be created by using a twin needle – refer to manufacturer's handbook for this method.

Tie quilting

A quick alternative to quilting is tying. A thicker, decorative thread, such as coton perlé, is used.

1 Start in the center of the place where you wish to position the tie. Taking the needle from the front to the back of the quilt, make a stitch through all three layers and draw the thread through, leaving a tail of about 6 in/15 cm. Take the needle back through to the reverse of the quilt in the same place as the first stitch and bring it back to the surface through the second hole. Draw the thread through and cut off leaving a tail of about 6 in/15 cm. Tie the two ends in a slip knot on the surface of the quilt (diagram 61).

diagram 61

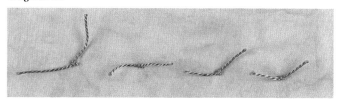

2 The technique for adding a button to the tie quilting is the same except the stitches are made through the holes of the button (diagram 62).

diagram 62

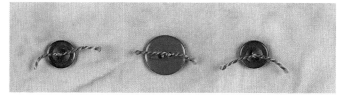

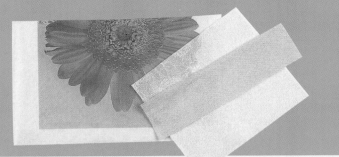

Gerbera Garden

Designed by Sarah Wellfair

The realistic flower images on this stunning quilt are photos of fresh gerberas printed onto fabric using a home printer. The floral squares are joined together with narrow sashing and the design is surrounded by a wide outer border, with more gerbera prints forming the four corner blocks. Simple flower motifs that echo the shape of the gerberas are quilted along the border, using multicolored thread.

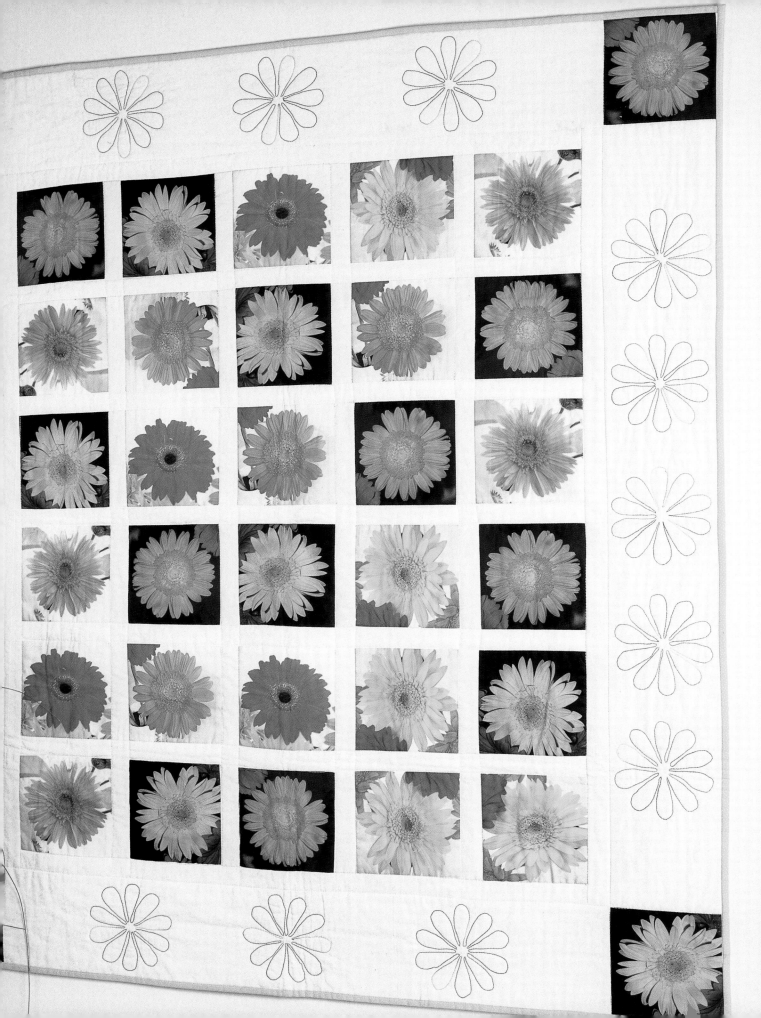

Finished size: 47 x 41 in/117.5 x 102.5 cm

MATERIALS

All fabrics used in the quilt top are 45 in/115 cm wide, 100% cotton

Sashing and borders: white-on-white print, 1½ yds/ 1.25 m

Backing: white-on-white print, 1¾ yds/1.50 m

Batting: 1¾ yds /1.50 m

Binding: Yellow spot print, 18 in/50 cm

Computer and printer

Sheet of letter paper, 8½ x 11 in

17 sheets of printable fabric (I used cotton poplin printable fabric by The Vintage Workshop, available online in 8 ½ x 11 in/21.5 x 28 cm sheets)

White thread for stitching and quilting

Water-soluble pen

Multicolored thread for quilting borders

ALTERNATIVE COLOR SCHEMES

1 Fields of flowers provide beautiful, natural patterns; 2 A collage of baby photos makes a marvelous heirloom quilt; 3 Photos from the family album make a wonderful memory quilt: you could even try printing modern photos in sepia tones to give the quilt a vintage look; 4 A selection of vacation photos will make a lovely reminder of countries and places visited.

1

2

3

4

PRINTING THE FLOWERS

1   Using a desktop publishing program or Photoshop software, download or scan your flower photos onto a computer. You will need at least six different photos to give you enough variation for the quilt design, which has 34 photos in total, 30 for the center of the quilt and four for the corners of the border. Alternatively, you could use a different flower for every photo.

2   Enlarge the photos to at least 5½ in/14 cm square – at this size, you should be able to get two of them onto an 8½ x 11 in sheet of letter paper. When you are satisfied with the photos, print trial images onto letter paper to make sure the range of colors is suitable for the quilt.

3   Now, following the manufacturer's instructions, print the photos onto the printable fabric. Cut them into 5½ in/14 cm squares and lay them out in six rows of five squares each.

CUTTING

1   From the 1⅜ yds/1.25 m of white-on-white fabric, cut five strips across the width of the fabric, 5½ in/ 14 cm deep. Cross-cut one of these strips into 24 pieces, 1½ in/4 cm wide for the short sashing.

2   From the remaining four strips, cut two strips, 31½ in/79 cm long for the top and bottom borders, and two strips, 37½ in/94 cm long for the side borders.

3   From the remainder of the white-on-white fabric, cut seven strips across the width of the fabric, 1½ x 29½ in/4 x 74 cm, for the horizontal sashing.

4   Then cut two further strips across the width of the white-on-white fabric, 1½ x 37½ in/4 x 94 cm, for the vertical sashing.

5   From the yellow spot print fabric, cut five strips across the width of the fabric, 2 in/5 cm deep, for the binding.

STITCHING

1   Take the 1½ x 5½ in/4 x 14 cm white-on-white strips and the flower blocks. Taking a ¼ in/0.75 cm seam allowance, pin and stitch six rows of five squares with a sashing strip between each square. Press the seam allowances towards the flower blocks.

2   Taking the usual seam allowance, pin and stitch five of the 1½ x 29½ in/4 x 74 cm white-on-white sashing strips between the rows, making sure the blocks are aligned (diagram 1). Add a further strip at the top and bottom of the rows. Press the seam allowances away from the sashing strips.

diagram 1

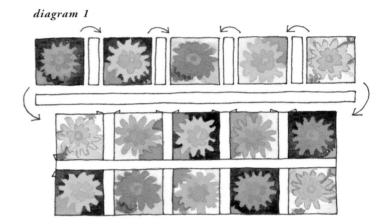

3   Taking the usual seam allowance, pin and stitch the 1½ x 37½ in/4 x 94 cm white-on-white vertical sashing strips to the sides. Press well.

ADDING THE BORDERS

1   Measure the pieced top through the center from top to bottom to make sure it is the same as the two 37½ in/94 cm borders and adjust the size of the border strips if necessary. Taking a ¼ in/0.75 cm seam allowance, pin and stitch the borders to the sides of the quilt. Press the seam allowances towards the border.

2   Take the two 31½ in/79 cm borders and, taking the usual seam allowance, stitch one flower block to each end of both borders. Press the seam allowances towards the border. Pin and stitch the borders to the top and bottom of the quilt, making sure you match the corners of the squares. Press the seam allowances towards the border.

Template actual size

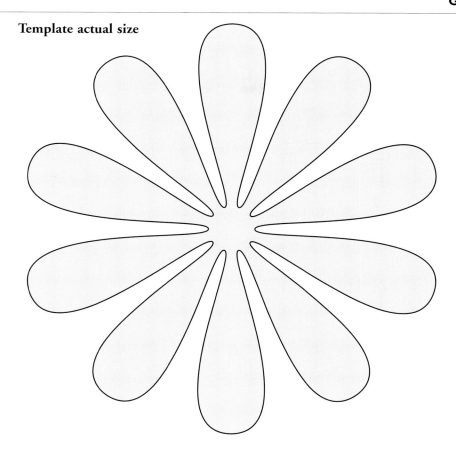

FINISHING

1   Remove the selvages from the backing and spread, right side down, on a flat surface, then smooth out the batting and the pieced top, right side up, on top. Fasten together with safety pins or baste in a grid.

2   Using white thread, quilt in-the-ditch (see page 9) around the squares and around the inner border. Trace the flower template above onto a piece of card and cut out. Transfer the flower shapes onto the borders by drawing around the card template with a water-soluble pen. Following the quilt plan on page 28, place three flowers equidistantly along the top and bottom, and five down the sides. Quilt around them with multi-colored thread.

3   Trim off any excess batting and backing so they are even with the pieced top. Join the yellow spot print binding strips with diagonal seams to make a continuous length to fit all around the quilt and use to bind the edges with a double-fold binding, mitered at the corners (see page 11).

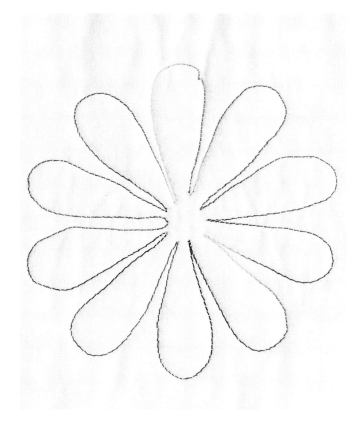

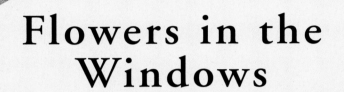

Flowers in the Windows

Designed by Janet Goddard

In this quilt, Attic Window blocks showcase all kinds of flowerpots, containing a variety of cleverly folded fabric flowers. The tactile, three-dimensional flowers, coupled with the bright color palette, create a vibrant wallhanging or a spectacular throw.

Finished size: 30½ x 42 in/76 x 105 cm

MATERIALS
All fabrics used in the quilt top are 45 in/115 cm wide, 100% cotton.

Background: cream print, 20 in/50 cm
Attic Window fabric 1: gold print, 4 in/10 cm
Attic Window fabric 2, outer border and binding: orange print, 30 in/76 cm
Pots, pitcher and sashing strips: turquoise blue, 20 in/50 cm
Stems and leaves: 6 in/15 cm each of two green prints

Flowers: 10 in/25 cm each of four fabrics – gold, yellow, peach and orange
Template plastic: 12 x 12 in/31 x 31 cm square
Fusible webbing: 20 in/50 cm
Neutral cotton thread for piecing
Threads to match fabrics for appliqué and flowers
Marking pencil
Six small peach and/or yellow buttons
30 yellow beads
Backing: 1½ yds/1.30 m
Batting: 80/20 cotton/polyester, 34 x 46 in/ 86 x 117 cm
Invisible thread and orange thread for quilting

ALTERNATIVE COLOR SCHEMES

1 The flowers here are made using the double button flower technique. They are stitched in shades of brown with bright yellow centers and beige buttons; 2 Double button flowers are shown here, too, stitched in red, white and green country checks with clear red buttons; 3 Using the yo-yo technique for making the flowers, this block has blue Attic Windows, a blue vase and pink flowers; 4 There are more yo-yo flowers on this block with green Attic Windows and shades of purple in the vase and flowers.

1

2

3

4

CUTTING

1   From the cream background print, cut six squares measuring $9\frac{1}{4}$ x $9\frac{1}{4}$ in/24 x 24 cm.

2   Using the template plastic, make either an imperial or a metric template of the Attic Window strip on page 39 (depending on which measurements you're using). Use the template to cut six strips from the gold print, then reverse it to cut six strips from the orange print.

3   From the turquoise blue fabric, cut three strips $10\frac{1}{2}$ x 2 in/27 x 5cm, four strips 22 x 2 in/56 x 5 cm, and two strips $36\frac{1}{2}$ x 2 in/93 x 5 cm.

4   From the orange print outer border fabric, cut four strips across the width of the fabric, $3\frac{1}{4}$ in/8 cm deep.

5   From the orange print binding fabric, cut four strips across the width of the fabric 2 in/5 cm deep.

NOTE   Instructions for cutting the folded flowers are given with the step-by-step instructions for each folding technique.

STITCHING THE ATTIC WINDOW BLOCKS

To make one block:

1   With right sides together, stitch a gold print strip to the right-hand side of a cream background square. Stop stitching $\frac{1}{4}$ in/0.75 cm away from the bottom (diagram 1a). Press the seam towards the strip.

diagram 1a

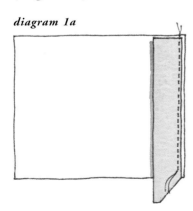

2   With right sides together, stitch an orange print strip to the lower edge of the cream background square. Stop stitching $\frac{1}{4}$ in/0.75 cm away from the corner. Press the seam towards the strip.

3   To complete the mitered corner, fold the block diagonally, right sides together, so that the strips are aligned and their angled edges meet. Stitch a diagonal seam into the corner. Press the seams towards the bottom (diagram 1b).

diagram 1b

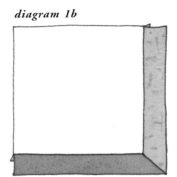

4   Repeat steps 1 to 3 to make six blocks in total.

PREPARING THE APPLIQUÉ

1   Trace the six pots and pitcher given on pages 39 to 41 onto the fusible webbing. Cut out roughly and iron to the reverse of the turquoise blue fabric. Cut out the shapes exactly along the marked lines.

2   Trace the required number of leaves and/or stems for each window onto the fusible webbing. Cut out and iron them to the reverse of the green fabrics, cutting three sets from one green fabric and three from the other.

3   Take a background Attic Window block and, removing the paper from the back of the appropriate pot, pitcher, stem and/or leaf, iron these onto the background to bond them in place. Use the quilt plan to determine the correct position and make sure that the vase is positioned directly on the orange strip.

4   Matching the thread to the fabric, work machine zigzag stitch around each shape and to add detail across the pots as indicated by the dotted lines on the templates.

5   Repeat steps 3 and 4 to make six blocks in total.

MAKING THE FLOWERS

The following instructions are for the folded flowers to be stitched to the Attic Window blocks. The gold, yellow, peach and orange fabrics are used for the flowers in a random way, so that each block has a range of colors. Choose the colors as you wish.

Yo-Yo Flowers

1   Make a plastic template of the yo-yo circle. Trace five circles onto the reverse of the flower fabric and cut out. Using a matching thread for each circle, turn under an ⅛ in/3 mm seam allowance to the reverse of the fabric all the way around the outer edge and work running stitch around it (diagram 2). Pull up the thread to gather the fabric, then secure the thread.

diagram 2

2   When all yo-yos are complete, position them in the vase and stitch them to the background with small slipstitches.

Folded Hexagons

1   Make a plastic template of both triangles. Using the large triangle template, trace and cut out one triangle from two different flower fabrics. Using the small triangle template, trace and cut out four triangles from one fabric and four triangles from another fabric.

2   Stitch two different-colored same-sized triangles right sides together, leaving a small opening. Trim the corners. Turn right side out and slipstitch the opening closed. Press.

3   Bring all three points together in the center of the triangle (diagram 3) and secure in place with a few stitches to make a folded hexagon.

diagram 3

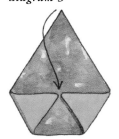

4   Repeat steps 1 to 3 until you have five folded hexagons in total. Position in the vase and stitch to the background with small slipstitches.

Spiraled Blooms

1   From the flower fabric cut three strips, 1⅛ x 20 in/3 x 50 cm. Take each fabric strip and press in half, wrong sides together, then open out and press each raw edge to the center.

2   Using a marking pencil, mark dots 1 in/2.5 cm apart, along one long edge of the strip. Turn the strip around and mark dots along the other edge but mark the first dot ½ in/1.25 cm in from the short end (diagram 4).

diagram 4

3   Take a knotted thread and, starting at one edge, secure the thread with two or three stitches. Stitch in an even running stitch from dot to dot, taking the thread over the edge of the fabric at the marked points. Stitch for about 5 in/13 cm, then begin to gather the fabric strip gently. Position the petals so that each row lies behind the previous row and keep gathering gently to create a flower shape. Continue stitching and gathering in this way until you reach the end of the strip. Secure the thread.

4   Starting in the middle of the flower, take a stitch through the base of the first six petals and gather tightly in a circle to form the center. Secure the first petal to the sixth petal. Tack the next petal slightly under the first and continue to tack petals to the back of the flower, just inside the edge. When you reach the end, taper the last petal under the flower and stitch in place.

5   Repeat steps 1 to 4 to make three blooms in total. Position the blooms in the basket and stitch to the background with small slipstitches.

Double Button Flowers

1 Make a plastic template of both the small and the large circles. Using the large circle template, trace and cut out three circles from the flower fabric. Using the small circle template, trace and cut out three circles from a contrasting flower fabric.

2 Mark the center of a circle with a cross. Fold over one edge of the circle to the center mark and press in place (diagram 5a). Working in a counterclockwise direction, fold over the next edge of the circle to the center as shown, and press (diagram 5b). Repeat four more times. Secure the center with a few stitches.

diagram 5a   *diagram 5b*

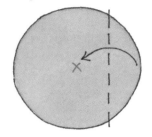   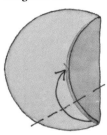

3 Repeat steps 1 and 2 to make three large and three small flowers in total.

4 Stitch a button to each of the small flowers, then stitch these to each of the large flowers. Position the flowers on the stems in the pot and slipstitch to the background.

Single Button Flowers

1 Using the large circle template and the method for the Double Button Flowers, make three flowers. Stitch a button to each large single flower.

2 Position the flowers on the stems in the pitcher and slipstitch to the background.

African Violets

1 Make a plastic template of the circle. Using this template, trace and cut out six circles from the flower fabric.

2 Using a matching thread for each circle, turn under an $\frac{1}{8}$ in/3 mm seam allowance to the reverse of the fabric all the way around the outer edge and work running stitch around it. Pull up the thread to gather the fabric, then secure the thread.

3 Bring up the needle with thread through the center of the gathered circle. Take a stitch from the center, over the outer edge and back up through the center. Pull tight. Repeat this four more times at even intervals. Secure with a couple of backstitches.

4 Stitch five yellow beads to the center of each African violet.

5 Position the flowers on the leaves and pot and slipstitch to the background.

ASSEMBLING THE BLOCKS

1 Following the quilt plan, lay out the blocks in three rows of two blocks. Taking a $\frac{1}{4}$ in/0.75 cm seam allowance, stitch a $10\frac{1}{2}$ x 2 in/27 x 5 cm turquoise blue strip between each pair of blocks. Press the seams towards the Attic Windows.

2 Taking the usual seam allowance, stitch a 22 x 2 in/56 x 5 cm turquoise blue strip between each pair of blocks, joining them together. Press the seams towards the turquoise blue strips. Stitch the remaining 22 x 2 in/56 x 5 cm turquoise blue strips to the top and bottom of the quilt.

3 Stitch the $36\frac{1}{2}$ x 2 in/93 x 5 cm turquoise blue strips to each side of the quilt.

ADDING THE BORDERS

1 Measure the pieced top through the center from side to side and cut two strips to this measurement from the $3\frac{1}{4}$ in/8 cm border strips. Taking a $\frac{1}{4}$ in/ 0.75 cm seam allowance, pin and stitch to the top and bottom of the quilt. Press the seam allowances towards the borders.

2 Measure the pieced top through the center from top to bottom and cut two strips to this measurement from the $3\frac{1}{4}$ in/8 cm border strips. Taking the usual seam allowance, pin and stitch to the sides of the quilt. Press the seam allowances towards the borders.

FINISHING

1 Remove the selvages from the backing and spread, right side down, on a flat surface, then smooth out the batting and the pieced top, right side up, on top. Fasten together with safety pins or baste in a grid.

2   Using the invisible thread, quilt in-the-ditch (see page 9) around each pot and flowers, background square and Attic Window strips.

3   Using the orange thread, quilt in a random square and line pattern around the outer border (diagram 6).

4   Trim off any excess batting and backing, so that they are even with the quilt top. Join the binding strips with diagonal seams to make a continuous length to fit all around the quilt and use to bind the edges with a double-fold binding, mitered at the corners (see page 11).

diagram 6

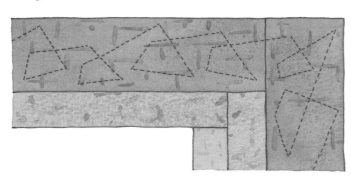

Templates all at 75%.
Enlarge on a photocopier by 133%.

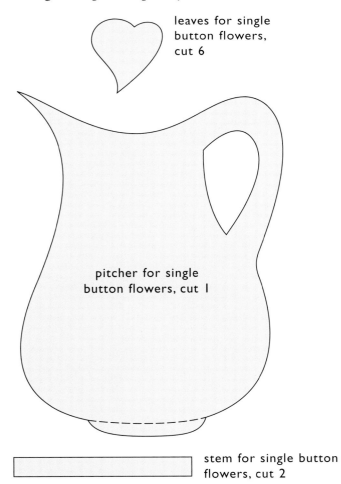

leaves for single button flowers, cut 6

pitcher for single button flowers, cut 1

stem for single button flowers, cut 2

stem for single button flowers, cut 1

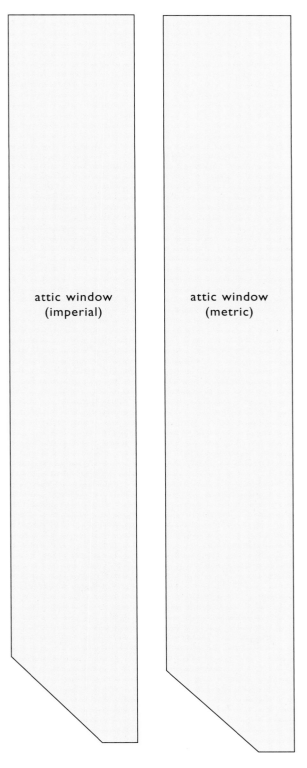

attic window (imperial)

attic window (metric)

Templates all at 75%. Enlarge on a photocopier by 133%.

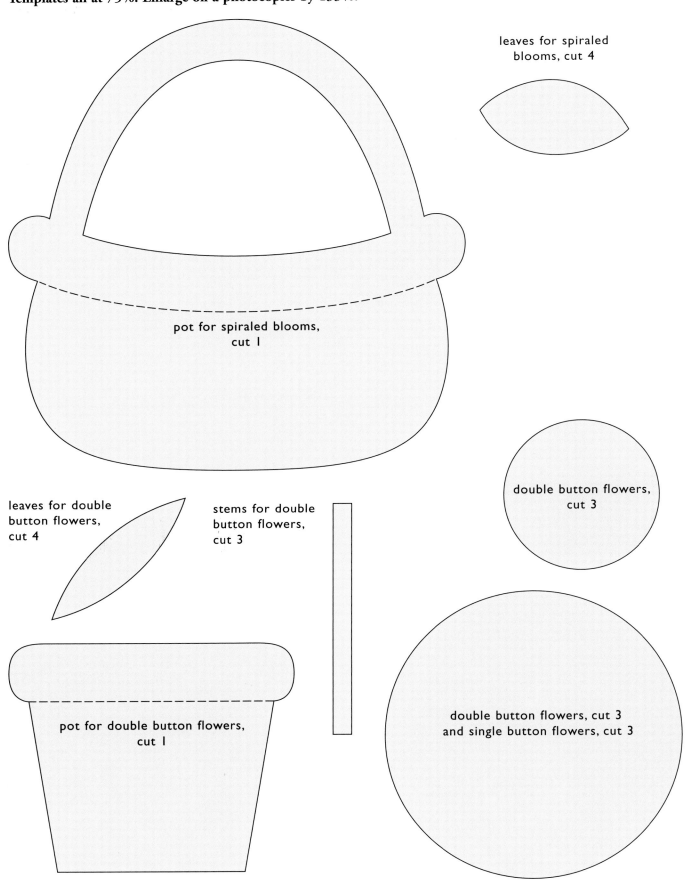

leaves for spiraled
blooms, cut 4

pot for spiraled blooms,
cut 1

double button flowers,
cut 3

leaves for double
button flowers,
cut 4

stems for double
button flowers,
cut 3

pot for double button flowers,
cut 1

double button flowers, cut 3
and single button flowers, cut 3

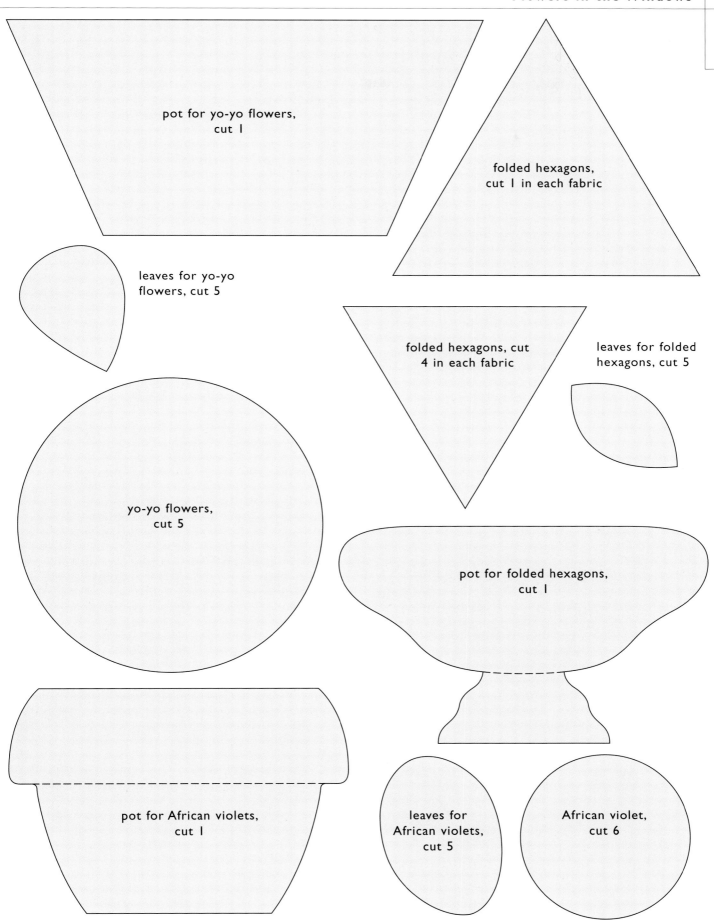

pot for yo-yo flowers,
cut 1

folded hexagons,
cut 1 in each fabric

leaves for yo-yo
flowers, cut 5

folded hexagons, cut
4 in each fabric

leaves for folded
hexagons, cut 5

yo-yo flowers,
cut 5

pot for folded hexagons,
cut 1

pot for African violets,
cut 1

leaves for
African violets,
cut 5

African violet,
cut 6

Circle of Pansies

Designed by Sarah Wellfair

This pretty wallhanging features the fascinating technique of flower crushing to produce a central image that's straight from nature. The rest of the patchwork is simply made up of two borders but could be made more complex with a series of borders if you prefer to make a larger piece.

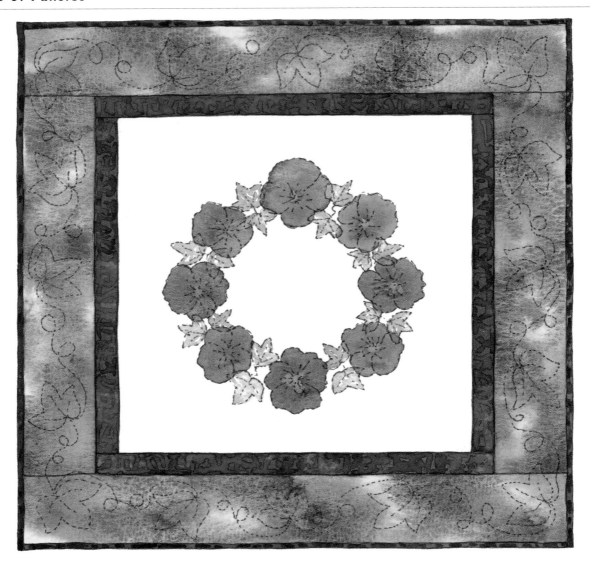

Finished size: 26 x 26 in/65 x 65 cm square

MATERIALS

All fabrics used in the quilt top are 45 in/115 cm wide, 100% cotton.

Do not buy the fabric for the borders and binding to match the color of the fresh flowers, as they change color after pounding. It is better to wait until you have seen the pounded color and then buy your fabrics.

Center panel: white fabric prepared for dyeing, 18 in/50 cm (available from quilt shops)

Inner border and binding: dark blue mottled fabric, 18 in/50 cm

Outer border: blue/green mottled fabric, 18 in/50 cm

Batting: 36 x 36 in/90 x 90 cm

Backing: 1 yd/1 m

Freezer paper: 1 yd/1 m

Dark felt-tipped pen

Masking tape

8 pansies

16 ivy leaves (variety of medium-sized and small ones)

Hammer

Quilting threads: kingfisher blue, yellow, olive green, white (or colors to suit your flowers)

ALTERNATIVE COLOR SCHEMES

1 The feathery purple and green leaves from an acer make a delicate design;
2 A ring of red rose petals makes a softly shaded pattern; 3 Holly leaves
arranged in a circle on a white-on-white print produce a good corner motif;
4 Aubretia petals scattered among beech leaves make a pretty combination.

1

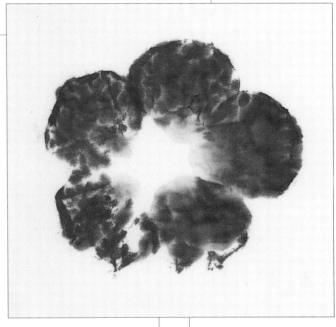

2

3

4

POUNDING THE FLOWERS

1 Cut a piece of white fabric for the center panel 17 x 17 in/43 x 43 cm square.

2 Cut a piece of freezer paper to the same size and place on the reverse of the white fabric with the shiny side down. Iron in place. This will act as a waterproof layer to prevent the flowers from dyeing your work surface.

3 Using a dark felt-tipped pen, draw a circle approximately 10 in/25 cm in diameter onto the paper side of the piece of freezer paper (I used a plate as a template). Turn the paper-lined fabric over and you should be able to see the circle through the fabric.

4 Using masking tape, tape the fabric, paper side down, onto the reverse of your cutting mat. Cut off the ivy leaf stalks and place eight pairs of leaves face down onto the fabric around the circle. Tape in place (diagram 1).

diagram 1

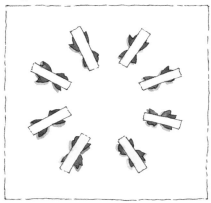

5 Next, place the pansies face down in between the leaves and tape in place (diagram 2).

diagram 2

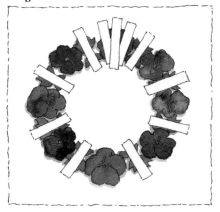

6 Cover the taped circle of pansies and leaves with another piece of freezer paper. Using the flat end of the hammer, pound the flowers and leaves until the flowers have almost disappeared, leaving their pigment in the fabric. The leaves will require more pounding as they take longer to dye the fabric and do not disintegrate in the same way as the pansies.

7 Gently remove the top freezer paper tape and any remaining particles of flowers or leaves. Peel the freezer paper off the back and leave the fabric to dry. Press the fabric on the wrong side with a hot iron to cure the flower dye – the flowers will have changed color as the pigments in the petals blended together.

8 Now that you can see the color of the flower dye, choose fabric for the borders and binding to match or contrast with it.

CUTTING

1 From the fabric chosen for the inner border, cut two strips, 1½ x 17 in/4 x 43 cm, for the side borders, and two strips, 1½ x 19 in/4 x 48 cm, for the top and bottom borders.

2 From the remainder of this fabric, cut four strips across the width of the fabric, 2 in/5 cm deep, for the binding.

3 From the fabric for the outer borders, cut two strips, 4 x 19 in/10 x 48 cm, for the side borders, and two strips, 4 x 26 in/10 x 65 cm, for the top and bottom borders.

4 Cut the backing fabric and batting to 28 x 28 in/71 x 71 cm square. From the backing fabric, cut a strip 24 x 5 in/61 x 12.5 cm for the hanging sleeve.

STITCHING

1 Taking a ¼ in/0.75 cm seam allowance, pin and stitch the two 1½ x 17 in/4 x 43 cm inner border strips to the sides of the center panel. Press the seams towards the borders.

2 Taking the usual seam allowance, pin and stitch the two 1½ x 19 in/4 x 48 cm inner border strips to the top and bottom of the center panel (diagram 3).

diagram 3

3   Then, taking the usual seam allowance, pin and stitch the two 4 x 19 in/10 x 48 cm outer border strips to the sides of the quilt. Press the seams towards the borders.

4   Finally, taking the usual seam allowance, pin and stitch the two 4 x 26 in/10 x 65 cm outer border strips to the top and bottom of the quilt (diagram 4).

diagram 4

FINISHING

1   Remove the selvages from the backing and spread, right side down, on a flat surface, then smooth out the batting and the pieced top, right side up, on top. Fasten together with safety pins or baste in a grid.

2   Using kingfisher blue thread, quilt around the pansy outlines. Then with yellow thread, quilt lines radiating out from the flower centers. Using olive green thread, quilt around the ivy leaves and along the leaf veins.

3   Changing to white thread, quilt the center of the flower ring heavily in a vermicelli pattern (see page 9). Quilt the background around the ring in the same pattern as the center but with the quilting lines slightly further apart.

4   Trace the ivy leaf design below onto freezer paper five times and cut out the leaf shapes. Iron the shapes onto one of the outer borders at equal intervals but turning them at random (diagram 5). Using the king-fisher blue thread, quilt around the leaves. Peel off the paper shapes and iron them onto the adjacent border, turning them at random as before. Repeat for the remaining two borders. Quilt the veins on the leaves, then quilt a random curling line to join the leaves.

Template actual size

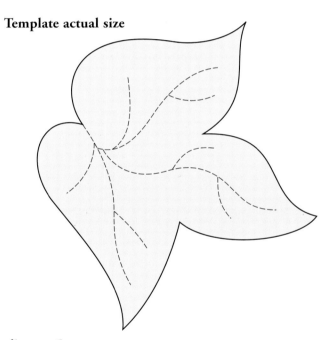

diagram 5

5   Trim off any excess batting and backing so they are even with the quilt top. Join the binding strips with diagonal seams and use to bind the edges with a double-fold binding, mitered at the corners (see page 11). Add a hanging sleeve, following the instructions in step 2 of "Finishing" on page 109.

Buttons and Blooms

Designed by Janet Goddard

This vintage quilt features delightful pots of flowers with button centers. Simple repeating squares show-case the 1930s reproduction fabric in pastel shades, while the buttons both embellish the quilt and hold the three layers of top, batting and backing together.

Finished size: 35½ x 41½ in/90 x 106 cm

MATERIALS

All fabrics used in the quilt top are 45 in/115 cm wide, 100% cotton.

Background: white print, 27 in/70 cm
Pots: peach print, 5 in/13 cm
Stems and leaves: green print, 5 in/13 cm
Squares: 4 in/10 cm each of eight print fabrics - light blue, medium blue, lilac, red, pink, peach and two shades of yellow

Fusible webbing: 20 in/50 cm
Border, backing and binding: green spot, 2 yds/1.80 m
Batting: 80/20 cotton/polyester blend, 38 x 44 in/ 97 x 112 cm
Buttons: 40 in a variety of pastel shades
Neutral cotton thread for piecing
White cotton thread for quilting
Threads to match fabrics for appliqué

ALTERNATIVE COLOR SCHEMES

Blocks 1 and 2 use country checks and plaids on a tea-dyed background fabric in colorways reminiscent of autumn; Blocks 3 and 4 use pastel pinks and blues with a hint of green for a color scheme inspired by spring.

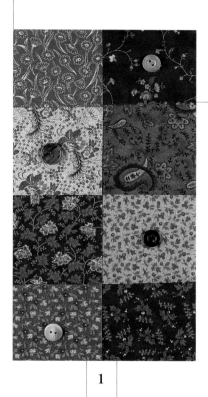

1

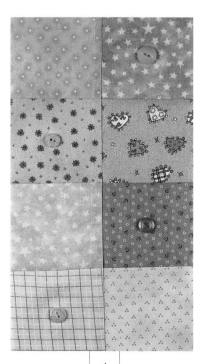

2

3

4

CUTTING

1 From the white background print, cut eight rectangles, 6½ x 12½ in/17 x 32 cm.

2 From each of the eight print fabrics, cut seven squares, 3½ x 3½ in/9 x 9 cm.

3 From the green spot fabric, cut four strips across the width of the fabric, 3 in/8 cm deep, for the border.

4 From the green spot fabric, cut five strips across the width of the fabric, 2 in/5 cm deep, for the binding. Use the remainder for the backing.

STITCHING

To make one pieced block:

1 Seven blocks of squares are needed for the quilt. Each block is made up of eight squares, one of each color. Taking a ¼ in/0.75 cm seam allowance, stitch the squares together in two rows of four. Press the seam allowances of one strip upwards and the seam allowances of the other strip downwards (diagram 1).

diagram 1

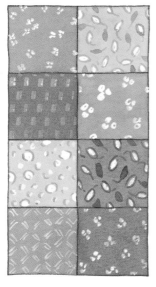

2 Taking the usual seam allowance and matching the seams, stitch the strips together. Repeat steps 1 and 2 to make seven blocks in total.

To make one appliquéd block:

3 Trace eight pots onto the fusible webbing. Cut out roughly and iron onto the reverse of the peach print fabric. Cut out the fabric pots exactly.

4 Trace eight blooms onto the fusible webbing. Cut out roughly and iron one bloom to the reverse of each of the eight print fabrics. Cut out the fabric blooms exactly.

5 Trace eight stems and 16 leaves onto the fusible webbing. Cut out roughly and iron onto the reverse of the green print fabric. Cut out the fabric stems and leaves exactly.

6 Take a white background print rectangle, remove the paper from the fused shapes, and iron one stem, two leaves, one pot and one bloom onto the background to bond them in place. Position the pot ¼ in/0.75 cm from the lower edge and overlap the ends of the stem with the pot and bloom (diagram 2).

diagram 2

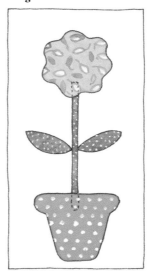

7 Matching the thread to the fabric, work machine zigzag stitch around each shape. Repeat steps 6 and 7 to make eight appliquéd blocks in total.

ASSEMBLING THE BLOCKS

1 Following the quilt plan on page 50, lay out the blocks in three rows of five, alternating a pieced block with an appliquéd block. Alternate the blocks row by row too.

2 Taking a ¼ in/0.75 cm seam allowance, pin and stitch the blocks together in horizontal rows. Press the seams towards the appliquéd blocks.

3 Taking the usual seam allowance and matching the seams, pin and stitch the rows together.

Templates all actual size

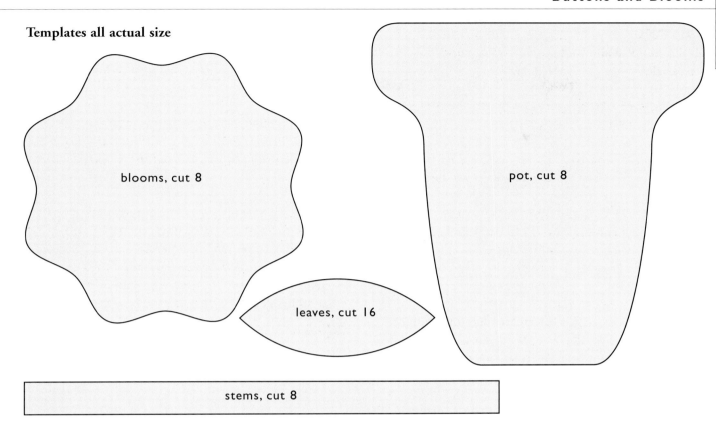

blooms, cut 8

pot, cut 8

leaves, cut 16

stems, cut 8

ADDING THE BORDERS

1 Measure the pieced top through the center from top to bottom, then cut two strips to this measurement from the 3 in/8 cm green spot border strips. Taking a ¼ in/0.75 cm seam allowance, pin and stitch to the sides of the quilt. Press the seam allowances towards the borders.

2 Measure the pieced top through the center from side to side, then cut two strips to this measurement from the 3 in/8 cm green spot border strips. Taking the usual seam allowance, pin and stitch to the top and bottom of the quilt. Press the seam allowances towards the borders.

FINISHING

1 Remove the selvages from the backing and spread, right side down, on a flat surface, then smooth out the batting and the pieced top, right side up, on top. Fasten together with safety pins or baste in a grid.

2 Using the white thread, quilt ¼ in/0.75 cm in from the outer edge of each appliquéd block.

3 Trim off any excess batting and backing so they are even with the quilt top. Join the binding strips with diagonal seams to make a continuous length to fit all around the quilt and use to bind the edges with a double-fold binding (see page 11).

4 Stitch a button to the center of each bloom and stitch a button to each alternate square (see page 17), ensuring that the colors of the buttons are randomly placed (diagram 3). Finally, stitch a button to each corner of the quilt on the border strip.

diagram 3

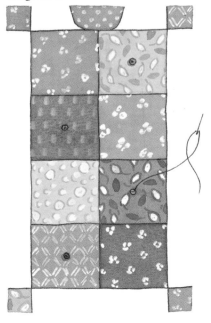

Autumn Kaleidoscope

Designed by Jane Coombes

The title of this quilt came about because the design resembles a kaleidoscope and the fabrics are representative of the changing colors of the leaves in autumn. It is made in a range of five fabrics that graduate from very dark to medium in tone. The seam lines are embellished with decorative machine embroidery in two shades: the darker thread on the medium-toned fabrics and the lighter thread on the darker fabrics.

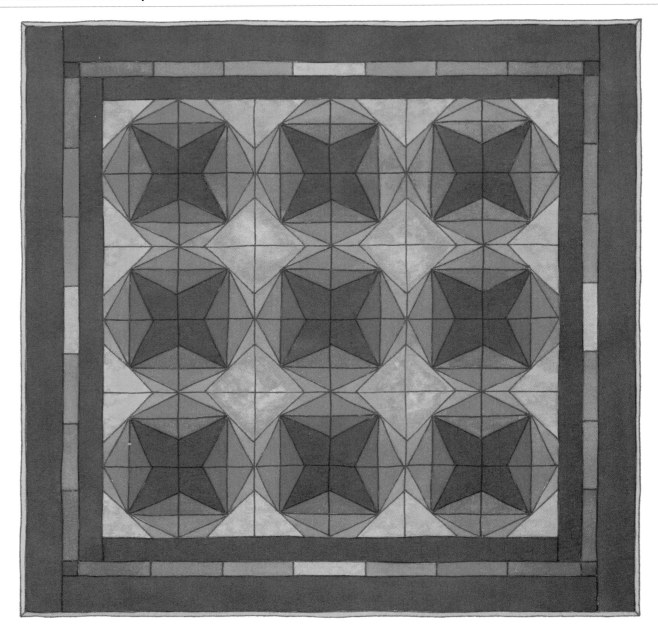

Finished size: 40 x 40 in/102 x 102 cm

MATERIALS
All fabrics used in the quilt top are 45 in/115 cm wide, 100% cotton.

Dark red: 1¼ yds/1 m
Red: ¾ yd/60 cm
Orange-red: ¾ yd/60 cm
Dark orange: ¾ yd/50 cm
Orange: 1 yd/80 cm
Foundation paper: 18 sheets **or lightweight sew-in interfacing:** 1 yd/1 m

Backing: 1¼ yds/1.10 m
Batting: 44 x 44 in/115 x 115 cm
Plain postcard and glue stick
"Add-a-quarter" and "Add-an-eighth" foundation piecing rulers
100% cotton thread for piecing
Invisible thread for quilting
Red and orange machine embroidery threads
Sewing machine with facility for decorative embroidery stitches

ALTERNATIVE COLOR SCHEMES

1 These fabrics are graduated from navy to very pale blue and the two decorative stitches used for embellishing are repeated symmetrically; 2 Here, the fabrics range in tone from dark to light and are embellished with a variegated thread; 3 A multi-colored print is selected for the two central sections of the block and a further two fabrics (purple and yellow) have been chosen to echo that color scheme; 4 In this neutral version, the fabrics vary from black to medium grey and include a silver section. The black section is embellished with silver metallic thread.

CUTTING

Cut the following strips across the width of the fabric:

1 From the dark red fabric cut:

a) six strips, 3 in/7 cm deep. Cross-cut the strips into 36 rectangles, 3 x 5¼ in/7 x 13.5 cm.

b) four strips, 2 in/5 cm deep, for the first border. Cut two of the strips to a length of 30½ in/79.5 cm and the remaining two strips to 33½ in/86.5 cm.

c) four squares, 1½ x 1½ in/4 x 4 cm, for the second border.

d) four strips, 3 in/7.5 cm deep, for the third border. Cut two of the strips to a length of 35½ in/91.5 cm and the remaining two strips to 40½ in/103.5 cm.

2 From the red fabric cut:

a) ten strips, 2 in/5 cm deep. Cross-cut the strips into 72 rectangles, 2 x 4½ in/5 x 11 cm.

b) two strips, 1½ in/4cm deep. Cross-cut the strips into eight rectangles, 1½ x 5¼ in/4 x 12 cm, for the second border.

3 From the orange-red fabric cut:

a) eight strips, 2½ in/6 cm deep. Cross-cut the strips into 72 rectangles, 2½ x 4 in/6 x 10 cm.

b) two strips, 1½ in/4 cm deep. Cross-cut the strips into eight rectangles, 1½ x 5¼ in/4 x 12 cm, for the second border.

4 From the dark orange fabric cut:

a) ten strips, 1½ in/4 cm deep. Cross-cut the strips into 72 rectangles, 1½ x 4½ in/4 x 11 cm.

b) two strips, 1½ in/4 cm deep. Cross-cut the strips into eight rectangles, 1½ x 5¼ in/4 x 12 cm, for the second border.

5 From the orange fabric cut:

a) three strips, 4¾ in/13 cm deep. Cross-cut the strips into 18 squares, 4¾ x 4¾ in/13 x 13 cm. Cut each square in half diagonally to make 36 half-square triangles.

b) one strip, 1½ in/4 cm deep. Cross-cut the strip into four rectangles, 1½ x 5¼ in/4 x 12 cm, for the second border.

c) five strips, 2¼ in/5.75 cm deep, for the binding.

WORKING THE FOUNDATION PIECING

1 Make a fabric code chart by cutting a small sample from each of the fabrics and sticking them with the glue stick to the postcard in a single column. Against each fabric, write the number of the section(s) for which that fabric is to be used, as follows: 1 – dark red; 2, 3 – red; 4,5 – orange-red; 6,7 – dark-orange; 8 – orange.

2 Enlarge the foundation pattern on page 61 (using either the imperial or metric version) and make 36 copies onto foundation paper or sew-in interfacing.

3 Position a dark red rectangle, right side uppermost, against the unmarked side of the foundation pattern, ensuring that the fabric overlaps the line between sections 1 and 2 by ¼ in/0.75 cm, and at the same time overlaps the remaining edges of section 1. Pin in position.

4 Place a red rectangle on top of the dark red rectangle, right sides together, matching the raw edges that are overlapping the line between sections 1 and 2 and the ends where the acute angles are towards the center of the block (diagram 1). Check that when this red rectangle is stitched along the solid line between sections 1 and 2 and flipped over, it will overlap the remaining edges of section 2 by at least ¼ in/0.75 cm on all sides.

diagram 1

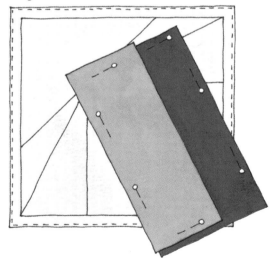

5 With the marked side of the foundation pattern uppermost, stitch along the line that divides sections 1 and 2 (diagram 2).

NOTE Use a small machine-stitch length to strengthen the seams and perforate the foundation pattern, enabling easier removal at a later stage.

diagram 2

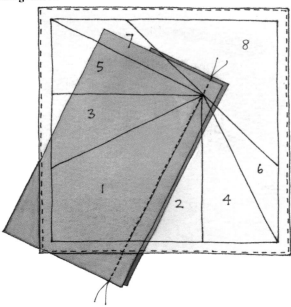

8 Turn the block over again so that the foundation pattern is uppermost. Carefully fold the foundation pattern back along the line that divides sections 1 and 3. Using the "Add-a-Quarter" ruler and a rotary cutter, trim the fabric overlap to ¼ in/0.75 cm (diagram 4a). Fold out the foundation pattern flat again (diagram 4b).

diagram 4a

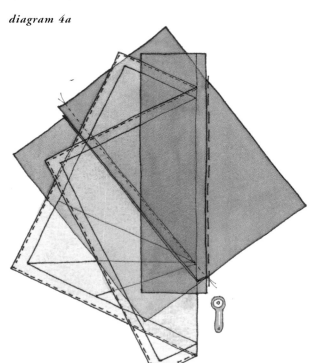

6 Fold back the foundation pattern along the stitched line and, using the "Add-an-Eighth" ruler and a rotary cutter, carefully trim the seam allowance to ⅛ in/0.4 cm (diagram 3).

diagram 3

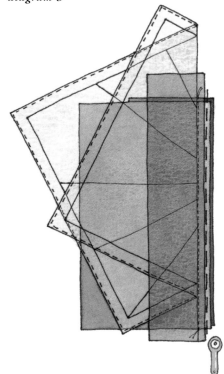

diagram 4b

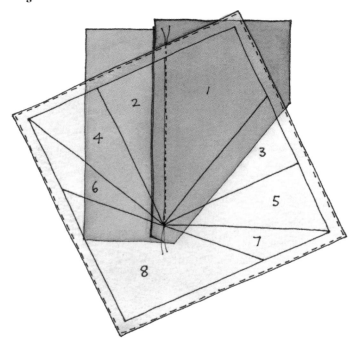

7 Turn the block over so that the fabrics are uppermost, flip the red fabric back into position and press lightly.

9 Turn the block over, fabric side uppermost. Position a red rectangle (for section 3), right sides together, along this pre-trimmed edge. Refer to step 4 if necessary.

10 Repeat steps 5-7, this time stitching between sections 1 and 3 (diagram 5).

diagram 5

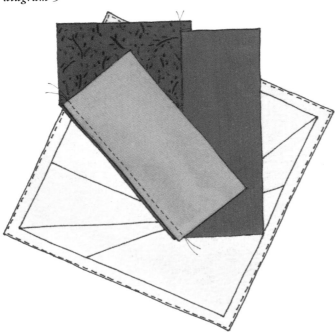

11 Referring to your fabric code chart for the colors of fabric to use, continue to stitch fabric pieces to the foundation pattern in numerical order, following these steps: trim overlap to ¼ in/0.75 cm; stitch; trim seam allowance to ⅛ in/0.4 cm; flip and press the fabric, until all sections are covered and the block is complete.

12 Trim the block seam allowances along the dotted lines of the foundation pattern. This completes one block. Repeat for the remaining 35 blocks.

JOINING THE BLOCKS

1 Taking a ¼ in/0.75 cm seam allowance and matching seams carefully, pin and stitch the blocks into pairs (diagram 6). Press the seam allowances to one side. Make 18 pairs in all.

diagram 6

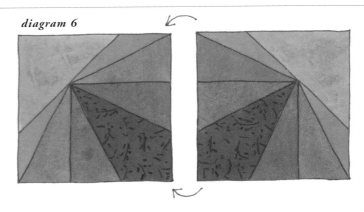

2 Pin and stitch the pairs into units of four blocks each and press the seam allowances as before (diagram 7). Make nine units in all.

diagram 7

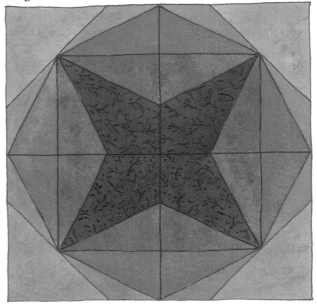

3 Following the quilt plan on page 56, pin and stitch these units into three rows of three units each. Press as before.

4 Pin and stitch the rows together to complete the central section of the patchwork and press as before.

ADDING THE BORDERS

1 To make the first border, use the 2 in/5 cm wide dark red border strips. Taking a ¼ in/0.75 cm seam allowance, pin and stitch the two shorter strips to the top and bottom of the quilt. Press the seam allowances towards the borders. Then pin and stitch the two longer strips to the sides of the quilt as before.

2 To make the second border, join the 1½ x 5¼ in/ 4 x 12 cm rectangles along their shorter edges in the following sequence (see also quilt plan): red, orange-red, dark orange, orange, dark orange, orange-red and red. Repeat four times to make four separate strips. Stitch a dark red square to each end of two of the strips. Stitch these strips to the quilt as in step 1, using the strips without the squares at each end as the shorter border strips.

3 To make the third border, use the 3 in/7.5 cm wide dark red border strips. Stitch these strips to the quilt as in step 1. Tear away the foundation papers, if used.

EMBELLISHING AND FINISHING

1 Remove the selvages from the backing fabric. Spread the backing right side down on a flat surface, then smooth out the batting and the patchwork top, right side up, on top. Fasten together with safety pins or baste in a grid.

2 Using a walking/even-feed foot on your sewing machine, quilt in-the-ditch (see page 9) along the seams joining the blocks, using invisible thread on the spool and 100% cotton thread to match the backing fabric in the bobbin.

3 Select an appropriate decorative machine embroidery stitch (a symmetrical style is preferable to one with a straight edge on one side). Using orange machine embroidery thread on the spool and cotton thread in the bobbin, stitch on the seam line around the outside edge of section 1 of each block to form a four-pointed star shape.

4 Select a different stitch and work along the seam lines between sections 2 and 4, and sections 3 and 5. Change to red embroidery thread, select two other stitches and work around the remaining seam lines of each block.

5 Using red machine embroidery thread, quilt the first border with a single line of straight stitching along the center. Work a single line of decorative stitching along the center of the second border. Quilt the third border with four lines of straight stitching, spaced the width of the walking foot apart.

6 Trim off any excess batting and backing so they are even with the quilt top. Join the binding strips with diagonal seams to make a continuous length to fit all round the quilt and use to bind the edges with a double-fold binding, mitered at the corners (see page 11).

Imperial template at 50%.
Enlarge on a photocopier by 200%

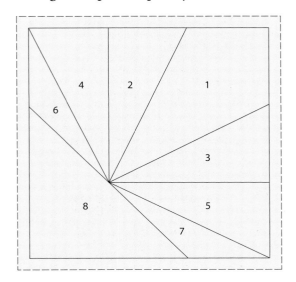

Metric template at 50%.
Enlarge on a photocopier by 200%

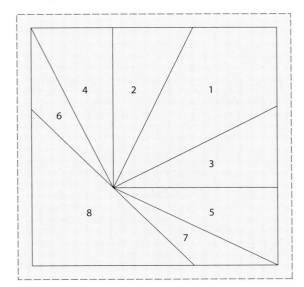

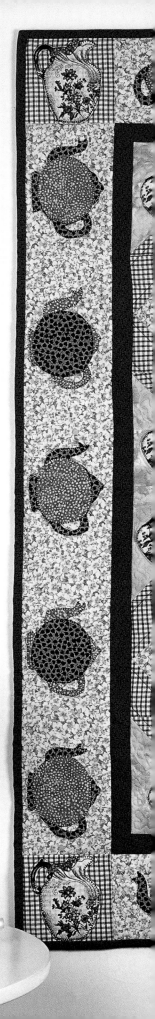

Afternoon Tea

Designed by Sarah Fincken

Childhood memories of long, hot summers, with tea and cake taken in the garden, triggered the idea of making a quilt that could be used on family picnics. A simple pieced block is used as a background to showcase broderie perse motifs of pitchers, cups and saucers, cut out from a treasured fabric. Appliqué teapots are added to the border to complement the theme. If you cannot find a fabric with suitable tea-time motifs, just use the templates provided to cut out the shapes from a fabric of your choice.

Finished size: 47 x 47 in/118 x 118 cm

MATERIALS

All fabrics used in the quilt top are 45 in/115 cm wide, 100% cotton, except the backing fabric which is 54 in/135 cm wide. Do not use striped or large checked fabric unless you are happy with the visually offbeat rhythm they will create on the quilt surface.

For the blocks:
Mottled pink fabric: 1 yd/1 m
Dark blue print: 1¼ yds/1.1 m
Blue check: ¾ yd /70 cm
Pink flower print: 1 yd/1 m

Tea-time or novelty fabric: ½ yd/50 cm
Blue spotted: ½ yd/50 cm
Blue leaf print: ½ yd/50 cm
Backing: 1½ yds/1.30 m, 54 in/135 cm wide
Batting: 80/20 cotton/polyester mix, 50 x 50 in/ 130 x 130 cm
Medium lead pencil
Fusible webbing: 2⅛ yds/2 m
Baking parchment
Pink and blue sewing thread
Invisible thread
White chalk marking pencil and ruler

ALTERNATIVE COLOR SCHEMES

1 A palette using soft golds, blue chintz and small check patterns gives an old-fashioned cottage garden feel to the block; 2 This vibrant color scheme featuring jazzy blue, green, red and orange patterns suggests the hues used in the china designs of Clarice Cliff from the 1930s; 3 A contemporary, bright scheme is suitable for a child's version of the quilt; 4 A contrasting combination of pinks and greens produces a bold, tropical effect.

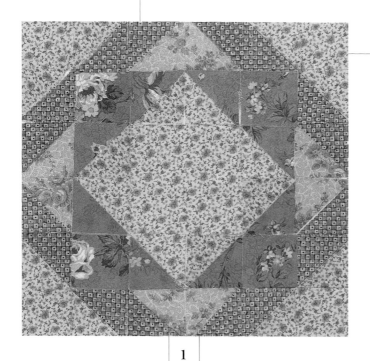

1

2

3

4

CUTTING
For the blocks:

1   From the mottled pink fabric, cut four strips, $3\frac{7}{8}$ in/10 cm deep, across the width of the fabric. Cross-cut the strips into 32 squares, $3\frac{7}{8}$ x $3\frac{7}{8}$ in/ 10 x 10 cm.

2   From the mottled pink fabric, cut two strips, $3\frac{1}{2}$ in/9 cm deep, across the width of the fabric. Cross-cut the strip into 16 squares, $3\frac{1}{2}$ x $3\frac{1}{2}$ in/9 x 9 cm.

3   From the mottled pink fabric, cut one strip, $6\frac{1}{2}$ in/16.5 cm deep, across the width of the fabric. Cross-cut the strip into four squares, $6\frac{1}{2}$ x $6\frac{1}{2}$ in/ 16.5 x 16.5 cm.

4   From the dark blue print, cut two strips, $3\frac{7}{8}$ in/ 10 cm deep, across the width of the fabric. Cross-cut the strips into 16 squares, $3\frac{7}{8}$ x $3\frac{7}{8}$ in/10 x 10 cm.

5   From the dark blue print, cut two strips, $3\frac{1}{2}$ in/ 9 cm deep, across the width of the fabric. Cross-cut the strips into 16 squares, $3\frac{1}{2}$ x $3\frac{1}{2}$ in/9 x 9 cm.

6   From the blue check, cut four strips, $3\frac{7}{8}$ in/10 cm deep, across the width of the fabric. Cross-cut the strips into 32 squares, $3\frac{7}{8}$ x $3\frac{7}{8}$ in/10 x 10 cm.

7   From the pink flower print, cut two strips, $3\frac{7}{8}$ in/10 cm deep, across the width of the fabric. Cross-cut the strips into 16 squares, $3\frac{7}{8}$ x $3\frac{7}{8}$ in/ 10 x 10 cm.

For the borders and binding:

1   From the dark blue print, cut four strips, $1\frac{1}{2}$ in/4 cm deep, across the width of the fabric for the inner border.

2   From the pink flower print, cut four strips, $4\frac{1}{2}$ in/11.5 cm deep, across the width of the fabric for the outer border.

3   From the blue check, cut four squares, $4\frac{1}{2}$ x $4\frac{1}{2}$ in/11.5 x 11.5 cm, for the border corners.

4   From the dark blue print, cut five strips, $2\frac{3}{4}$ in/7 cm deep, across the width of the fabric for the binding.

For the backing:
Cut a piece of backing fabric, 50 x 50 in/130 x 130 cm.

MAKING THE HALF-SQUARE TRIANGLE UNITS

1   For half-square triangle unit 1, take 16 mottled pink squares, $3\frac{7}{8}$ x $3\frac{7}{8}$ in/10 x 10 cm and 16 dark blue squares, $3\frac{7}{8}$ x $3\frac{7}{8}$ in/10 x 10 cm. Place a mottled pink square right sides together with a dark blue square, matching the raw edges exactly.

2   Using a medium lead pencil and ruler, draw a line diagonally from corner to corner on the pink square. Stitch $\frac{1}{4}$ in/0.75 cm on either side of the marked line (diagram 1).

diagram 1

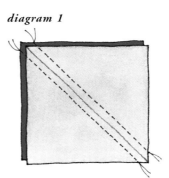

3   Cut the square in half along the marked line to make two half-square triangle units. Open out and press the seam allowances towards the darker fabric (diagram 2). Trim off the triangular "ears."

diagram 2

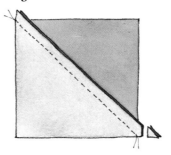

4   Repeat steps 1 to 3 using the remaining 15 mottled pink squares and 15 dark blue squares to make a total of 32 mottled pink/dark blue half-square triangle units.

NOTE When you are stitching a lot of half-square triangle units, use the chain piecing method for speed (see page 7).

ASSEMBLING A BLOCK

1 Following the block layout in diagram 3, lay out all the half-square triangle units needed for one block on your work surface. You will need eight units from each of set 1, set 2 and set 3 per block.

5 For half-square triangle unit 2, take 16 pink flower squares, 3⅞ x 3⅞ in/10 x 10 cm and 16 blue check squares, 3⅞ x 3⅞ in/10 x 10 cm. Repeat the method given in steps 1 to 4 to make a total of 32 pink flower/blue check half-square triangle units.

2 Place a 6½ in/16.5 cm mottled pink square in the center, then fill the gaps with four dark blue and four mottled pink 3½ in/9 cm squares.

3 Taking a ¼ in/0.75 cm seam allowance, stitch the units together in rows. Press the seam allowances opposite ways in alternate rows. Then pin and stitch the rows together, matching the seams, to complete the first block. Press the seam allowances open. Repeat steps 1 to 3 to make three more blocks.

6 For half-square triangle unit 3, take 16 mottled pink squares, 3⅞ x 3⅞ in/10 x 10 cm and 16 blue check squares, 3⅞ x 3⅞ in/10 x 10 cm. Repeat the method given in steps 1 to 4 to make a total of 32 mottled pink/blue check half-square triangle units.

4 Taking the usual seam allowance, pin and stitch the blocks together in pairs. Press the seam allowances open. Then join the pairs of blocks, matching the seams. Press the seam allowances open.

diagram 3

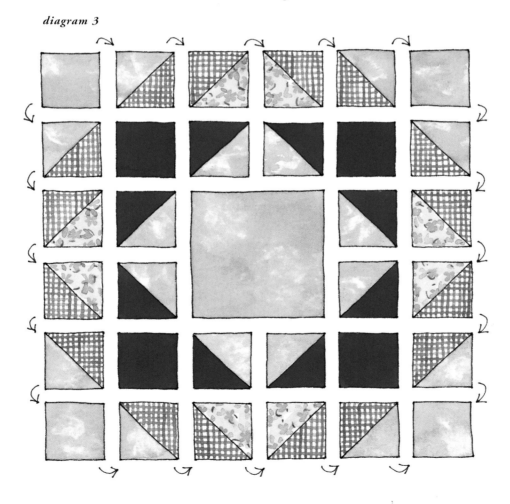

ADDING THE BORDERS

1 Measure the pieced top through the center from top to bottom and from side to side – it should measure 36½ x 36½ in/91.5 x 91.5 cm. Square it up if necessary.

2 Cut two dark blue 1½ in/4 cm inner border strips to this measurement. Taking a ¼ in/0.75 cm seam allowance, pin and stitch the strips to the top and bottom of the quilt. Press the seam allowances towards the borders.

3 Measure the pieced top through the center from top to bottom, then cut the two remaining dark blue 1½ in/4 cm inner border strips to this measurement. Taking the usual seam allowance, pin and stitch to the sides of the quilt. Press the seam allowances towards the borders.

4 Measure the pieced top through the center from side to side. Cut two of the pink flower print outer border strips to this measurement – it should be 38½ in/96.5 cm. Taking the usual seam allowance,

Templates all actual size

teapot: cut knob, handle, spout and base in one fabric and pot in a contrasting fabric – cut 20 of each

small pitcher

small pitcher

large pitcher

pin and stitch to the top and bottom of the quilt. Press the seam allowances towards the borders.

5   Cut the other two pink flower print outer border strips to 38½ in/96.5 cm. Taking the usual seam allowance, stitch a 4½ in/11.5 cm blue check square to each end of the two strips. Press the seam allowances towards the squares.

6   Taking the usual seam allowance, pin and stitch the borders to the sides of the quilt, matching the seams at the corners. Press the seam allowances towards the borders.

ADDING THE APPLIQUE EMBELLISHMENT

1   If you are not using a novelty fabric with tea-time motifs, trace the templates for the pitchers given below. Transfer eight large pitcher shapes and 16 assorted smaller pitcher shapes onto the paper side of the fusible webbing and cut out roughly. Remember to mirror-image your pattern if you want some of the pattern shapes to be reversed. Iron the fusible webbing onto the back of the novelty fabric and cut out the pitcher shapes exactly on the marked lines. If using tea-time fabric, simply iron fusible webbing behind the shapes, then cut out the motifs.

2   Repeat to cut out 16 cups and saucers from the novelty fabric, and 20 teapots with contrasting bodies from the blue spotted and blue print fabrics.

3   Remove the backing paper from the appliqué shapes. Following the quilt plan on page 64, iron the shapes in place on the patchwork top, covering them with baking parchment first to protect your iron. Using a matching pink or blue sewing thread, work machine zigzag stitch around each shape.

FINISHING

1   Remove the selvages from the backing and spread, right side down, on a flat surface, then smooth out the batting and the pieced top, right side up, on top. Fasten together with safety pins or baste in a grid.

2   Using invisible thread in the needle and a matching sewing thread in the bobbin, quilt in-the-ditch (see page 9) around the blocks and inner border.

3   Mark the quilt top with the desired geometric quilting lines with a ruler and chalk marking pencil. Machine quilt, using blue sewing thread in the needle and pink thread in the bobbin.

4   Using pink thread and a large, open vermicelli stitch (see page 9), quilt all over the mottled pink areas. Outline all the teapots about ⅛ in/0.3 cm away from the edge.

5   Trim off any excess batting and backing so they are even with the quilt top. Join the binding strips with diagonal seams to make a continuous length to fit all around the quilt and use to bind the edges with a double-fold binding, mitered at the corners (see page 11).

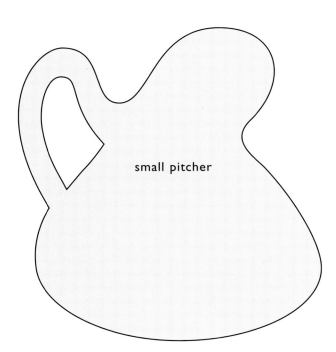

small pitcher

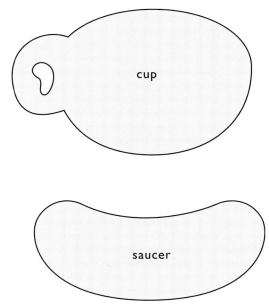

cup

saucer

Crazy Patchwork Wallhanging

Designed by Nikki Foley

Traditional crazy quilts were made in various ways, a popular method being to stitch randomly shaped patches to large square blocks. The patches were embroidered and embellished with ribbon and braid, then joined with or without sashing. This wall quilt reflects the tradition of crazy patchwork, while giving it a modern twist with crazy patchwork borders and prairie points.

Finished size: 43 x 58 in/108.5 x 146.5 cm (without prairie points)

MATERIALS
Crazy patchwork blocks and borders: approximately 9 in/23 cm each of at least seven patterned and plain fabrics in green, sand and cream. Any weight of fabric can be used, including cotton, curtain fabric and upholstery fabric. The different textures of these materials will add to the decorative feel of the crazy patchwork.
Foundation fabric: lightweight calico, 1½ yds/1.35 m, 60 in/150 cm wide

Borders and prairie points: sand-colored chintz, 1½ yds/1.35 m, 54 in/135 cm wide
Assorted braids, ribbons or other embellishments: approximately 4 yds/3.75 m in total
Embroidery threads, both hand and machine: in complementary colors, such as gold, cream and sand
Batting: 45 x 60 in/115 x 155 cm
Backing: 1¾ yds/1.60 m, 60 in/150 cm wide, in color of your choice
7 curtain rings with clips for hanging (can be purchased from a good haberdashery store) **or**
6 x 42 in/15 x 110 cm extra of backing fabric to make a hanging sleeve

ALTERNATIVE COLOR SCHEMES

1 Black and purple change the look of the crazy quilt completely, giving the design a dramatic impact; 2 Pinks and whites for all the girls: this is a perfect centerpiece for a young girl's bedroom; 3 Try incorporating a feature fabric into the design – these trucks or tractors will keep any little boy happy; 4 Tiny floral and gingham checks give a lovely country feel.

1

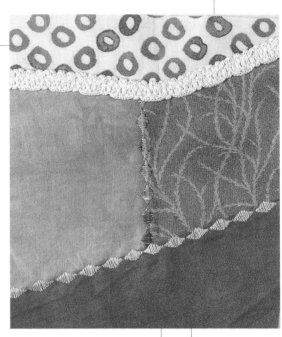

2

3

4

CUTTING

1 From the lightweight calico, cut two strips, 11½ in/29 cm deep, across the width of the fabric. Cross-cut the strips into six squares, 11½ x 11½ in/ 29 x 29 cm, for the foundation squares.

2 From the lightweight calico, cut four strips, 4½ in/11.5 cm deep, across the width of the fabric. Cut two of the strips into 50½ in/128 cm lengths for the side foundation borders. Cut the remaining two strips into 43½ in/110 cm lengths for the top and bottom foundation borders.

3 From the chintz, cut six strips, 5½ in/14cm deep, across the width of the fabric for the sashing. Cross-cut one of the strips into three 10½ x 5½ in/27 x 14 cm rectangles. From the remaining four strips, cut two 25½ in/64 cm lengths, two 40½ in/103 cm lengths and two 35½ in/90 cm lengths.

4 From the chintz, cut two strips, 7 in/18 cm deep, across the width of the fabric. Cross-cut the strips into eight squares, 7 x 7 in/18 x 18 cm, for the prairie points.

WORKING THE CRAZY PATCHWORK

1 Cut a piece from one of the green fabrics in a random shape, big enough to cover the corner of a calico foundation square. Place in position on the calico, right side up. Cut a second irregular patch from a different fabric and in a different shape, and place it, also right side up, next to the first patch, overlapping the raw edges by no more than ½ in/1.5 cm. Pin in place (diagram 1).

diagram 1

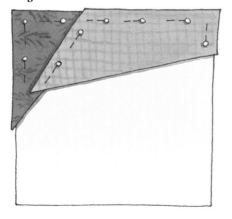

2 Continue cutting and overlapping different fabrics, right side up, pinning them down as you go, until the whole foundation square is covered. Make sure that you cut an interesting variety of shapes and that the same fabrics do not touch within the block. Trim back any large overlaps to about ½ in/1.5 cm.

3 Using large tacking stitches, stitch the pieces onto the foundation square along the overlapped seams to hold them in place until they are secured with decorative stitches or braids (diagram 2).

diagram 2

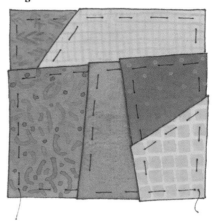

4 Now begin to cover the raw edges of the overlapping patches in various ways. You can use a zigzag or decorative machine stitch. Alternatively, stitch some of the seams by hand, using embroidery stitches such as the buttonhole stitch, cross stitch or herringbone stitch (see pages 15 and 16). Another way to embellish your crazy patchwork is with braid or ribbon, but limit this to three or four pieces per square. Pin the braid or ribbon over some of the seams, ensuring that it covers both overlapping edges. Then stitch down both sides of the braid using a straight stitch.

5 Continue embellishing the seams until they are all covered. Repeat with the remaining five squares. When you have completed all six crazy patchwork squares, press them gently from the back and trim to 10½ x 10½ in /27 x 27 cm.

6 Now cover the four calico foundation strips for the borders with crazy patchwork in the same way, starting at one end and working your way along to the other end.

STITCHING

1   Following the quilt plan on page 72 and using a ¼ in/0.75 cm seam allowance, pin and stitch one of the 10½ x 5½ in/27 x 14 cm chintz sashing pieces between two of the crazy patchwork squares. Repeat with the remaining two sashing pieces and four crazy patchwork squares to make three rows of two squares each. Press the seams towards the sashing.

2   Lining up the squares carefully, pin and stitch the three rows together with a 25½ x 5½ in/64 x 14 cm sashing strip between each one. Press the seams towards the sashing.

3   Now pin and stitch a 40½ x 5½ in/103 x 14 cm sashing strip to either side of the central panel. Press the seams towards the sashing.

4   Pin and stitch a 35½ x 5½ in/90 x 14 cm sashing strip to the top and bottom of the central panel. Press the seams towards the sashing. Trim away any excess sashing.

ADDING THE BORDERS

1   Measure the pieced top through the center from top to bottom, then trim the two 50½ in/128 cm crazy patchwork border strips to this measurement. Taking a ¼ in/0.75 cm seam allowance, pin and stitch to the sides of the quilt. Press the seams towards the borders.

2   Measure the pieced top through the center from side to side, then trim the two 43½ in/110 cm crazy patchwork border strips to this measurement. Taking the usual seam allowance, pin and stitch to the top and bottom of the quilt. Press the seams towards the borders. Trim any excess border fabric.

MAKING THE PRAIRIE POINTS

1   Take one of the 7 in/18 cm squares and, with wrong sides together, fold it in half diagonally and in half again to make a triangular shape (see page 12). Press. Repeat with the remaining seven squares to make a total of eight prairie points.

2   With raw edges matching, pin the prairie points along the bottom of the quilt, pointing upwards. Place the first one aligned with the side edge, then overlap the next one by about 1 in/2.5 cm. Continue overlapping the prairie points until you have placed all eight

of them, ensuring that the last one is aligned with the opposite edge (diagram 3). Take a look at the points and check they are overlapped evenly – adjust if necessary.

diagram 3

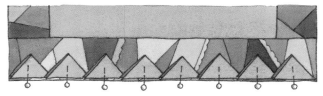

3   When you are happy with the arrangement of the prairie points, pin, then tack them in position ¼ in/0.75 cm away from the raw edge.

FINISHING

1   Spread the pieced top face up on a flat surface and smooth it out. Remove the selvages from the backing and lay face down on top, smooth it out and trim it to the same size. Lay the batting on top of the backing and, again, smooth and trim. Pin all around the edges.

2   Starting half-way down one side and taking a generous ¼ in/0.75 cm seam allowance, stitch all the way around the four sides, leaving a 12 in/30 cm gap on one side for turning through. Take care when sewing through the prairie points, as the layers will make the quilt quite thick here. Carefully trim across the quilt corners to remove bulk.

3   Turn the quilt right side out and smooth out the layers, rolling the edges out so that the seam lies just underneath the edge. Pin along the opening. If the prairie points are still pointing upwards, gently press them down with an iron. Pull out any tacking stitches. Pin and baste the layers together, smoothing them out as you go.

4   Using a thread to match the borders, stitch ¼ in/0.75 cm away from the edge of the quilt, sewing the opening together when you get to it.

5   Using a matching thread, just quilt over the chintz sashing strips with angled lines that reflect the crazy patchwork pattern.

6   To hang, either clip on the curtain rings and hang the quilt on a curtain pole mounted onto the wall or make a hanging sleeve (see step 2 of "Finishing," page 109).

Flying Geese and Roses

Designed by Sheilah Daughtree

This throw features three different types of blocks: a pieced flying geese pattern, a woven ribbon design and roses embroidered in silk ribbon. The designs are unified by the cream background and are all made from harmonious tones of pink and purple. The designs take a little time to complete but are not complicated and the result is well worth the effort.

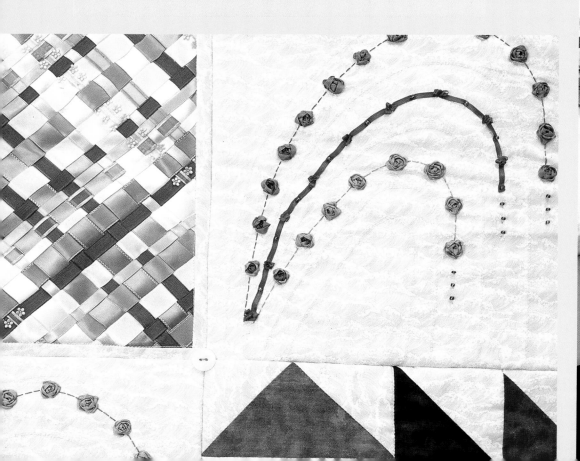

Finished size: 54 x 74 in/135 x 185 cm

MATERIALS
All fabrics used in the quilt top are 45 in/115 cm
wide, 100% cotton.

Flying Geese blocks:
pinks and mauves to match border, 24 squares of
assorted fabrics, 6¼ x 6¼ in/16 x 16 cm;
cream tone-on-tone* for background, 1 yd/75 cm;
thin, soft batting**, 1 yd/85 cm, 45 in/115 cm wide
Ribbon Roses blocks:
soft satin or silk ribbon, ⅛ in/3-4 mm wide:
 dark mauve 37 yds/34 m,
 light mauve 40 yds/37 m,
 crimson 31 yds/29 m;
cream tone-on-tone* for background, 1¾ yds/1.50 m;
calico for backing, 1¾ yds/1.50 m;
thin, soft batting**, 1¾ yds/1.50 m, 45 in/115 cm wide
Woven Ribbon blocks:
cream tone-on-tone*, ½ yd/50 cm;
iron-on interfacing, ¾ yd/60 cm, 36 in/90 cm wide;
¾ in/2 cm ribbon in assorted pinks, a total of
45 yds/42 m;

½ in/1.25 cm ribbon in assorted pinks, a total of
16½ yds/15.25 m;
thin, soft batting**, ¾ yd/70 cm, 45 in/115 cm wide
Batting: thin, soft batting**, 54 x 74 in/
135 x 185 cm for backing
Backing and border: pink pattern, 2¼ yds/2 m,
60 in/150 cm wide
Threads: monofilament thread; stranded embroidery
cotton
Paper: 29 sheets thin 11 x 17 in paper (optional)
Fade-away pen
Embellishments: assorted small glass beads; 24 cream
¾ in/2 cm buttons; 3 decorative 1¼ in/3 cm buttons
Cork board or ironing board
Blunt-ended tapestry needle or satay stick: for ribbon
weaving
Teflon sheet or baking parchment: for pressing
woven ribbons
Spray adhesive

* **Total cream tone-on-tone required**: 3¼ yds/3 m
Total batting required: 90 x 108 in/222 x 270 cm
(queen size). Use a fine poly/cotton batting rather
than 100% cotton which would be too heavy.

ALTERNATIVE COLOR SCHEMES

These variations show alternative ideas for the different block designs.
1 Flying Geese blocks arranged to make a diamond and embellished
with a button in the center; 2 Beads embroidered in a spiral to echo
the fabric pattern; 3 Simple running stitch embroidery with tiny
decorative buttons; 4 Flying Geese blocks highlighted with an outline
of stitching in metallic thread.

1

2

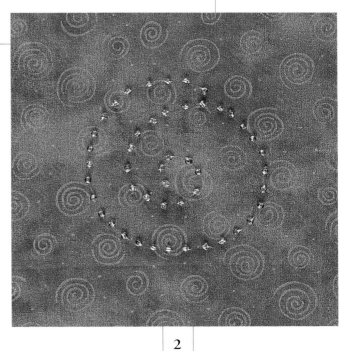

3

4

CUTTING

1 If using a queen-sized piece of batting, cut a piece 56 x 76 in/140 x 190 cm before cutting the smaller squares. This large piece is needed for the back of the quilt.

2 Cut the backing into a piece measuring 59 x 79 in/147.5 x 197.5 cm.

FLYING GEESE BLOCKS

1 Cut each 6¼ in/16 cm colored square across both diagonals to give four triangles (total of 96 large triangles).

2 From the cream tone-on-tone, cut nine strips, 3⅞ in/8.75 cm deep, across the width of the fabric. Cross-cut into a total of 96 squares, 3⅞ x 3⅞ in/8.75 x 8.75 cm. Cut each square across one diagonal to give two triangles (total of 192 small triangles).

3 Sew a small triangle to each short side of a large triangle to give a total of 96 Flying Geese units (diagram 1). Press the seam allowances towards the darker fabric.

diagram 1

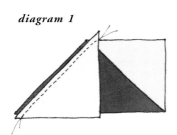

4 Join the units in pairs, varying the color combinations (diagram 2). Join the pairs into units of four and then into eight to complete the block (diagram 3). Press the seams towards the large triangle points. A total of 12 Flying Geese blocks is needed.

diagram 2

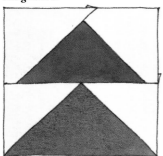

diagram 3

5 Cut the batting into twelve 11 in/27.5 cm squares and tack or pin to the back of each block. Using monofilament thread, quilt in-the-ditch (see page 9) around each triangle.

NOTE If your machine catches on the batting, back the block with thin paper and tear away after stitching.

6 Trim the blocks to 10½ in/26.25 cm square and set aside.

RIBBON ROSES BLOCKS

1 From the cream tone-on-tone fabric, cut five strips, 11 in/27.5 cm deep, across the width of the fabric. Cross-cut into 17 squares, 11 x 11 in/27.5 x 27.5 cm.

2 Using the fade-away pen, trace template 1 on page 83 for the off-center design. Trace template 2 on page 83 for the symmetrical design, repeating it as a mirror image to complete the design.

3 Take one of the background squares and place it over one of the off-center designs on a light box or taped onto a window, making sure to line up the cross on the template with the center of your fabric. Using the fade-away pen, transfer the design and mark the placement of the roses (1 in/2.5 cm apart). Repeat with the remaining background squares, tracing 14 off-center designs and three symmetrical designs.

4 Cut the calico into 11 in/27.5 cm squares as in step 1. Tack a square of calico to the back of each cream tone-on-tone square to give it a body. Using one strand of stranded embroidery cotton to match your ribbon, stitch a Y-shape with three stitches ¼ in/0.75 cm long at the first "rose" position. Then add two more stitches to make a five-pointed star – this makes a regular base for weaving the ribbon, called a "spider's web" (diagram 4).

diagram 4

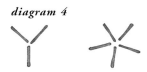

5 Cut a length of ⅛ in/3-4 mm wide soft satin or silk ribbon – each rose takes about 9 in/22 cm of ribbon. Thread the ribbon into a tapestry needle and bring the needle through from the back, but do not knot the ribbon at the back. Weave the ribbon over and under the "spider's web" until a rose is formed (diagrams 5a and 5b).

diagram 5a

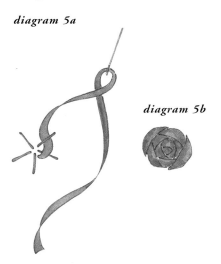

diagram 5b

6 Take the ribbon back through the fabric, underneath the rose and cut, leaving a ½ in/1.25 cm tail. Using sewing thread, stitch the two loose ends flat. If you wish, add a small bead or French knot in a contrasting color to the center of the rose.

7 Repeat steps 4 to 6 to make more roses along the design line. Then, using two strands of stranded cotton, work the stems in large running stitches. Add three small beads to the end of each line.

8 To make the line of mock ribbon roses in the middle of the off-center designs, mark the curve at 1 in/2.5 cm intervals to place the mock roses, then thread a needle with ⅛ in/3-4 mm wide soft satin or silk ribbon and a second needle with sewing thread in a matching color.

9 Bring the silk ribbon up at the base of the curve. Bring the sewing thread up at the first marked point, then make 4 or 5 gathering stitches in the ribbon. Pull up the gathers and make a small stitch through them to secure to the background. Repeat to make a line of mock roses. Cut off the ribbon and tuck under the last rose, securing with a few little stitches.

10 Add batting as in step 5 of the Flying Geese block instructions. Using a twin needle and cream thread, echo the curves of the design, about ½ in/ 1.25 cm away.

11 Trim as for Flying Geese, step 6, and set aside. Repeat for the remaining Ribbon Roses blocks.

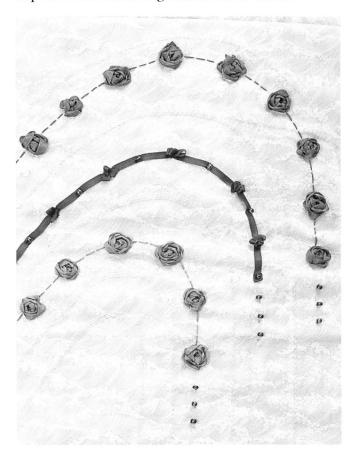

WOVEN RIBBON BLOCKS

1   Cut the iron-on interfacing into six 10 in/25 cm squares. Place one of these squares onto a cork board or ironing board, glue side up. Pin all four corners, with pins angled outwards. Cut the ribbons into varying lengths as required.

2   Lay the first ribbon corner to corner across the diagonal and pin at an angle at each end, so that the pins hold the ribbon firmly stretched out. Working either side of the central ribbon, lay different-colored and different-width ribbons parallel to it and pin until the interfacing is covered (diagram 6).

diagram 6

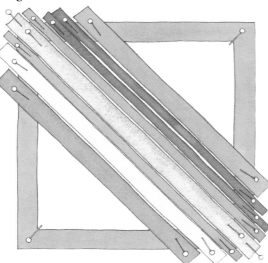

3   Starting at the center and using a blunt-ended tapestry needle (or satay stick), weave a ribbon at right angles in and out of the pinned ribbon. Pin each end at an angle as before (diagram 7). Adjust where necessary so that the lines are straight and the weave firm.

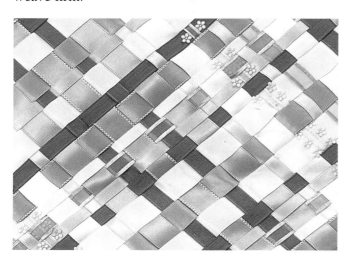

diagram 7

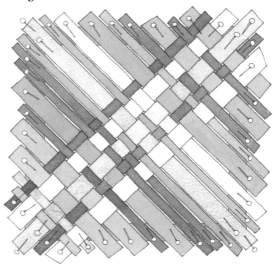

4   Place the Teflon sheet or baking parchment on top of the ribbons and press with an iron to fuse the ribbons to the interfacing. Remove the pins and trim to 9¼ in/24 cm square.

5   From the cream tone-on-tone fabric, cut four border strips, 1½ x 10½ in/4 x 26.5 cm wide for each Woven Ribbon block. Stitch four border strips around the block Log Cabin style (diagram 8).

diagram 8

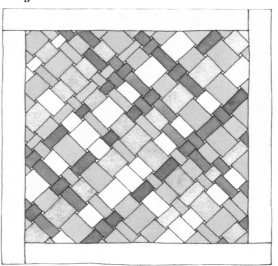

6   Before adding the batting as in step 5 of the Flying Geese block instructions, spray sparingly with adhesive on one side. Place the Woven Ribbon block, right side up, on top of the sticky side of the batting and trim as for Flying Geese, step 6.

7   Repeat steps 1- 6 to make six Woven Ribbon blocks in total. Set aside.

FINISHING

1   Following the quilt plan on page 78, lay out the blocks in the correct order. Using a ¼ in/0.75 cm seam allowance, pin and stitch the blocks into rows. Press the seam allowances in different directions on alternate rows. Then pin and stitch each row together, matching the seams carefully.

2   Spread the backing piece, right side down, on a flat surface, then smooth out the batting and the pieced top, right side up, centrally on top. Fasten together with quilter's safety pins. The backing will be brought around to the front to make the borders.

3   Stitch a cream button at each corner where the blocks meet, and a decorative button on each central symmetrical Rose block (see page 17).

4   Using the fade-away pen, draw a line on the batting around the quilt top, 2 in/5 cm away from the quilt top edge. Folding the backing out of the way, cut only the batting to this line. Then re-position the edge of the backing.

5   Turn in and press ½ in/1.5 cm all round the edge of the border. Then fold again to make the border 2 in/5 cm wide, and pin onto the quilt top, leaving the corners free for a short distance each way.

6   The Japanese-style folded corners are pinned separately (diagram 9). Cut away the corner batting.

Templates at 50%.
Enlarge on a photocopier by 200%

diagram 9

Open up the righthand side border, then fold the corner down over the top border to form a right angle and pin.

7   Now fold the side border on top of the pinned corner, previously folded. Repeat for the other corners.

8   Using monofilament thread in the bobbin and cream thread on top, work blind hem stitch around the border to secure it. Hand-stitch the corners.

NOTE   The folded corner technique used for the border of this quilt was first developed by Kumiko Sudo.

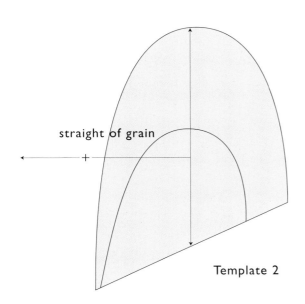

straight of grain

Template 2

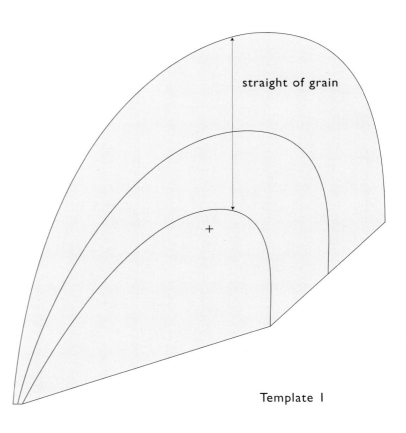

straight of grain

Template 1

Licorice Allsorts

Designed by Nikki Foley

This funky quilt is made with hand-dyed fabric and black fabric strips, embellished with buttons and strands of knobbly wool. It is an eye-catching project that will brighten up your life and look good wherever you choose to put it. Any bright fabrics, especially batiks, would work well for the quilt, if you don't want to dye your own.

Finished size: 59½ x 69½ in/142.5 x 166.5 cm

MATERIALS
All fabrics used in the quilt top are 45 in/115 cm wide, 100% cotton.

If dyeing your own fabric:
Blocks: plain white cotton fabric suitable for dyeing (check with the retailer if the fabric needs pre-washing or soaking before you start), 2 yds/2 m
Inner border: plain white cotton fabric (as above), 28 in/75 cm
Dyes: one box each of red, yellow, blue, turquoise and purple cold-water dyes

> **NOTE** Make sure you read all the instructions that come with the product to ensure you have a good understanding of the health and safety aspect of using dyes. Always wear gloves and work in a well-ventilated area.

Strong plastic bags (good-quality, medium-sized freezer bags would be ideal)
If buying pre-colored fabric:
Blocks: batiks or similar in orange, red, blue, green, turquoise, purple, yellow and pink (or any combination of eight bright colors of your choice), 8 in/20 cm of each color
Inner border: very bright yellow fabric, 28 in/70 cm

You also need:
Blocks, outer border and binding: black fabric, 2¾ yds/2.40 m
Backing: 3½ yds/3.30 m in color of your choice
Batting: 64 x 74 in/162 x 188 cm
Selection of brightly colored buttons (68 in total)
1 ball of knobbly wool

ALTERNATIVE COLOR SCHEMES

Any color goes with black. You can have great fun embellishing the black and trying out lots of different colors. 1 How about lime green and black, embellished with some purple and green twine?; 2 Pink and black, with some very fashionable fluffy wool, make an interesting combination; 3 Adding blue, or a combination of blues, creates a very dramatic quilt; 4 Multi-colored fabrics, with strips of black added, give the design an ethnic feel.

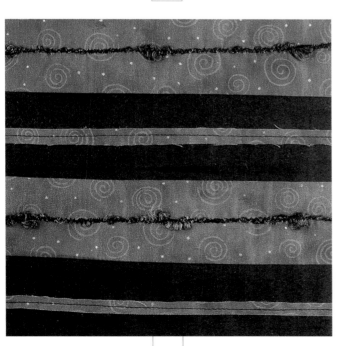

1

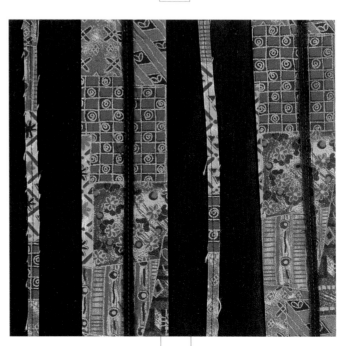

2

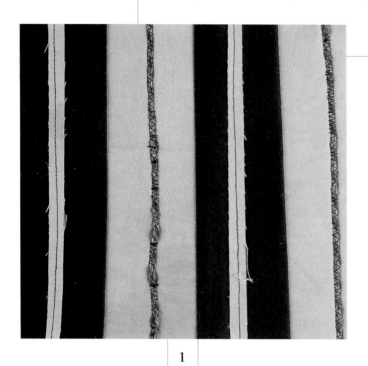

3

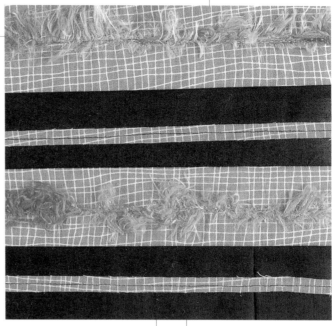

4

CUTTING AND DYEING

1 If you are dyeing your own fabric, wash it first to remove any finishing or treatments if necessary. Leave to dry.

2 From the white cotton fabric, cut eight strips across the width of the fabric, 8 in/20 cm deep.

3 Follow the manufacturer's instructions for mixing the dyes. Cover a large table or other work surface with sheets of plastic, such as garbage bags. If it is the right weather, a garden table outside is a good idea.

4 Put one of the 8 in/20 cm strips of white cotton onto the covered surface and, using the color guide at right, pour over the first color, i.e. yellow. Don't pour on too much – the fabric needs to be colored all over with the dye but not dripping.

5 Take the next color, i.e. red, and use an old spoon or yoghurt cup to dribble it over the top of the first color. You should apply the second color more sparingly than the first. The second color will run and start to spread over the first, but don't worry – that's meant to happen. Add a third color if there is one listed on the color guide. The fabric should now be visibly wet with dye. If you feel it is not wet enough, pour on a little more of the first color.

6 Now scrunch up the fabric, place it into a plastic bag and tie the top of the bag loosely. Wipe the plastic surface clean. Continue dyeing the remaining white cotton fabric strips, working through the color guide and placing each piece in a separate plastic bag.

7 If you want to dye the inner border, take the 28 in/71 cm piece of white fabric and completely cover it with yellow dye. Then drop tiny amounts of all the other colored dyes over it and place it in a separate plastic bag.

8 Leave the fabrics in a warm place for the recommended time. Then rinse them thoroughly until the water runs clear. Hang the fabrics up and, when they are nearly dry, press them with an iron.

NOTE If you decide to do more dyeing for your quilt-making, you will find that your fabrics will turn out very differently each time. There are many ways to create original patterns – the best way to find out is to experiment with color and techniques. If you are particularly interested, there are many books available that cover the subject in more depth.

COLOR GUIDE

First color	Second color	Third color	End result
YELLOW	RED		ORANGE
YELLOW	BLUE		GREEN
YELLOW	TURQUOISE	BLUE	SEA GREEN
TURQUOISE	BLUE		BRIGHT BLUE
TURQUOISE	BLUE	RED	DARK BLUE/PURPLE
RED	BLUE		PURPLE
RED	YELLOW	TINY BIT OF BLUE	DARK ORANGE
2 PARTS YELLOW	I PART RED		DEEP YELLOW

CUTTING

1 From the black fabric, cut 16 strips across the width of the fabric, 3 in/7.5 cm deep, for the blocks.

2 Also from the black fabric, cut 16 strips, 2½ in/ 6 cm deep, across the width of the fabric. Put these strips to one side for the outer border and binding (eight strips for each).

3 From each of the eight colored fabrics, cut two strips, 3 in/7.5 cm deep, and two strips, ½ in/1.5 cm deep, for the blocks. Keep the strips together in color groups – you will have 16 colored strips 3 in/7.5 cm wide and 16 colored strips ½ in/1.5 cm wide.

4 From the bright yellow fabric, cut eight strips, 3 in/7.5 cm deep, across the width of the fabric for the inner border.

5 Cut the backing in half crossways and remove the selvages.

STITCHING

1 Take two 3 in/7.5cm strips of the black fabric and two 3 in/7.5 cm strips of one of the colored fabrics. Taking a ¼ in/0.75 cm seam allowance, stitch them together, alternating the black and colored strips. Iron all the seam allowances towards the black fabric.

2 Lay a length of knobbly wool along the center of each colored strip and pin it into position. Using a matching thread, couch in place by working machine zigzag stitch over the top of the wool (diagram 1).

diagram 1

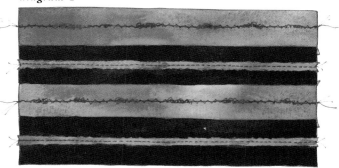

3 Now lay a ½ in/1.5 cm strip of matching colored fabric along the center of each black fabric strip (diagram 1). Using a matching thread, work straight machine stitch along the middle of the colored strips, attaching them to the black strips. Don't worry if the colored strips start to fray – don't trim them at this stage.

4 Cross-cut the strip set into four squares, 10½ x 10½ in/25.5 x 25.5 cm.

5 Repeat steps 1 to 4 with each set of colored strips. You need 30 blocks in total.

6 Following the quilt plan on page 86, lay out the blocks, alternating vertical and horizontal strips throughout the quilt. Check the positions of the blocks to make sure the colors are distributed in a pleasing way.

7 Taking a ¼ in/0.75 cm seam allowance, pin and stitch the blocks into six rows of five blocks each. Press all the seams open. (Take care when ironing the knobbly wool as many modern wools are polyester based and will melt if the iron is too hot.)

8 Taking the usual seam allowance and matching seams, pin and stitch the six rows together. Press the seams open.

ADDING THE BORDERS

1 To make the inner border, measure the pieced top through the center from side to side, then join two strips of the yellow border fabric and cut to the right length. Taking a ¼ in/0.75 cm seam allowance, pin and stitch to the top and bottom of the quilt. Press the seam allowances towards the borders.

2 Measure the pieced top through the center from top to bottom, then join two strips of the yellow border fabric and cut to the right length. Taking the usual seam allowance, stitch to the sides of the quilt. Press the seam allowances towards the borders.

3 To make the outer border, repeat steps 1 and 2 using the 2½ in/6 cm black border strips.

FINISHING

1 Stitch the backing into one piece down the long sides. Spread right side down on a flat surface, then smooth out the batting and the patchwork top, right side up, on top. Fasten together with safety pins or baste in a grid.

2 Using a matching thread, quilt by working machine zigzag stitch along both sides of the ½ in/ 1.5 cm colored strips that are stitched onto the black strips. The colored strips are meant to remain slightly frayed, so keep the stitching away from the frayed edge but trim off any very long threads.

3 Sew brightly colored buttons to the corners of each block and evenly spaced out along the black borders (see page 17).

4 Trim off any excess batting and backing so that they are even with the quilt top. Join the black binding strips with diagonal seams to make a continuous length to fit all around the quilt and use this to bind the edges with a double-fold binding, mitered at the corners (see page 11).

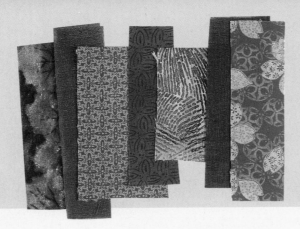

Orient Quilt

Designed by Gail Smith

The rich colors of the fabrics used in this quilt remind me of the fabulous array of fragrant spices to be found in any Oriental market. The golden yellow, strong green and warm reds are perhaps colors that you would not normally put together, but in this case each fabric complements the other (just like the spices in a curry). The fabric is manipulated into pintucks which form natural channels for the bead embellishment.

Finished size: 49 x 43 in/123.5 x 108.5 cm

MATERIALS

All fabrics used in the quilt top are 45 in/115 cm wide, 100% cotton, except the cotton lamé, which has some nylon in it.

Yellow ocher: 25 in/64 cm
Japanese floral red/gold print: 15 in/38 cm
Dark red print: 15 in/38 cm
Pink/gold multi print: 24 in/61 cm
Green cotton lamé: 6 in/15 cm
Red cotton lamé: 15 x 12½ in/38.5 x 32 cm
Sashing/borders: dark green print, 1½ yds/1.40 m (allow more for a directional print)

Backing: 1¼ yds/1.20 m, 60 in/150 cm wide, in color of your choice
Batting: low loft, 52 x 45 in/132 x 115 cm
Binding: Japanese red/gold mini print: ½ yd/50 cm
Fusible webbing: 12 in/30 cm
Selection of machine embroidery threads, including red and gold metallic
Fancy yarn for couching
Chunky red Aran wool or similar for decorative cords
Red stranded embroidery cotton
8 red buttons
Small gold beads
16 medium-sized red beads

ALTERNATIVE COLOR SCHEMES

These alternative color schemes are inspired by other parts of the world: 1 The red, white and blue is striking and would suit a masculine decor; 2 Icy blue and silver reminds me of the frozen landscapes of the Antarctic; 3 This lush green color scheme works well even though the fabrics come from a similar color group; 4 Turquoise blues and yellows make a fresh, crisp combination.

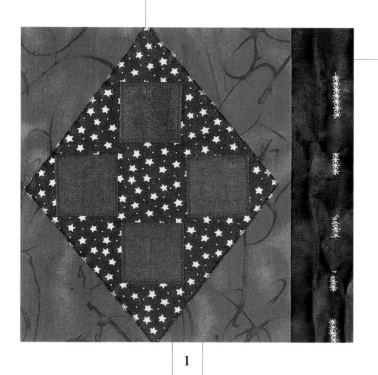

1

2

3

4

CUTTING

1 From the yellow ocher, cut four blocks, 14½ x 12½ in/37 x 32 cm.

2 Cut the 15 in/38 cm pieces of the Japanese floral red/gold print and the dark red print in half along the crease from the bolt.

3 On a large piece of paper, draw a rectangle measuring 14 x 12 in/35.5 x 30.5cm. Mark the mid-point along each edge, then join up the points to form a diamond (diagram 1). Cut out the diamond and use as a template to cut four diamond shapes from the pink/gold multi print.

diagram 1

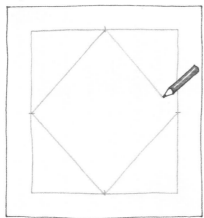

4 Iron fusible webbing onto the back of the green cotton lamé, then cut out 16 squares, 3 x 3 in/ 7.5 x 7.5 cm.

5 From the dark green print fabric, cut four strips down the full length of the fabric, 2 in/5 cm wide, for the borders. Cut two strips down the full length of the fabric, 2½ in/6.5 cm wide, for the vertical sashing. Cut six strips, 2½ x 12½ in/6.5 x 32 cm, for the horizontal sashing

6 From the Japanese red/gold mini print, cut five strips, 2½ in/6.5 cm deep, across the width of the fabric for the binding.

MAKING THE PINTUCKS

1 Take the pieces of the Japanese floral red/gold print and the dark red print. Pin narrow tucks ³⁄₁₆ in/ 5 mm deep along the length of the fabric, from top to bottom, placing them at approximately 1½ in/4 cm intervals. Stitch along the pinned lines to form pin-

tucks (diagram 2). Trim the pintucked strips to make four blocks 14½ x 12½ in/37 x 32 cm. Make pintucks along the piece of red cotton lamé in the same way to make a fifth block.

diagram 2

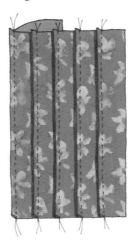

2 Using red machine embroidery thread, stitch horizontal lines across the Japanese floral red/gold print blocks approximately 2½ in/6.5 cm apart, pressing the pintucks to alternate sides as you go (diagram 3).

diagram 3

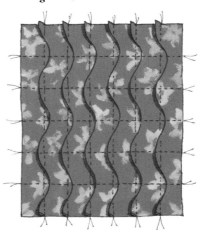

3 On the red cotton lamé block, use gold machine embroidery thread to stitch decorative machine stitches between the pintucks.

BEGINNING THE EMBELLISHMENTS

Some of the embellishments are added at this stage. Further embellishments will be added later, at the quilting stage.

1 On the dark red cotton print blocks, use a narrow machine zigzag stitch to couch curving lines of fancy yarn in between alternate pairs of pintucks.

2   Pin the four pink/gold multi print diamond shapes in the center of the four yellow ocher blocks, then work straight machine stitch round the edges.

3   Cut lengths of chunky red Aran wool or similar, long enough to go around the edges of the diamonds. Using machine zigzag stitch, catch the wool down to form decorative machine cords (diagram 4).

diagram4

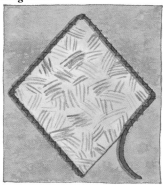

4   Take the 16 green cotton lamé squares prepared earlier and position one square in each corner of the diamonds. Using a protective cloth, fuse in place with an iron.

5   Iron fusible webbing onto the back of the remaining Japanese floral red/gold print. Cut into 16 squares $1\frac{3}{4}$ x $1\frac{3}{4}$ in/4.5 x 4.5 cm. Fuse the squares in place on the green lamé squares, tilting them on point. Work machine zigzag stitch around both the green and the Japanese squares (diagram 5).

diagram 5

ADDING THE SASHING AND BORDERS

1   Check the sizes of your blocks before proceeding – they should measure $14\frac{1}{2}$ x $12\frac{1}{2}$ in/37 x 32 cm. Trim carefully to size if necessary.

2   Following the quilt plan on page 92, lay out the blocks in three rows of three blocks. Taking a $\frac{1}{4}$ in/0.75 cm seam allowance, pin and stitch a short horizontal dark green sashing strip between the blocks to make three columns. Press the seam allowances towards the sashing.

3   Taking the usual seam allowance and matching the blocks carefully, pin and stitch two long dark green sashing strips in between the blocks.

4   Measure the pieced top through the center from side to side, then cut two of the dark green border strips to this measurement. Taking the usual seam allowance, pin and stitch the border strips to the top and bottom of the quilt. Press the seam allowances towards the borders.

5   Measure the pieced top through the center from top to bottom, then cut two of the dark green border strips to this measurement. Taking the usual seam allowance, pin and stitch to the sides of the quilt. Press the seam allowances towards the borders.

FINISHING

1   Remove the selvages from the backing and spread, right side down, on a flat surface, then smooth out the batting and the pieced top, right side up, on top. Fasten together with safety pins or baste in a grid.

2   Using gold metallic machine embroidery thread, quilt just inside the blocks and around the diamonds. Then, on the dark red print blocks, quilt wavy lines between alternate pairs of pintucks.

3   Use red stranded embroidery cotton to "tie" the red buttons through all layers at each corner and on the long vertical sashing (see page 25).

4   On the dark red print blocks, add small gold beads along the pintucks (see page 18). Stitch a medium-sized red bead to the center of each small diamond on the yellow ocher blocks.

5   Trim off any excess batting and backing so they are even with the quilt top. Join the binding strips with diagonal seams to make a continuous length to fit all around the quilt and use to bind the edges with a double-fold binding, mitered at the corners (see page 11).

Isle of Skye Quilt

Designed by Gail Smith

I have always been drawn to things nautical and love seascapes. I am sure this is because my mother was born on the beautiful Isle of Man and took us there every year for our summer vacation. The seaside is the inspiration for this abstract quilt. Horizontal bands of fabric in shades of blue and sand are enhanced with many different embellishments, including couched threads, hand stitching, ruffles and beads.

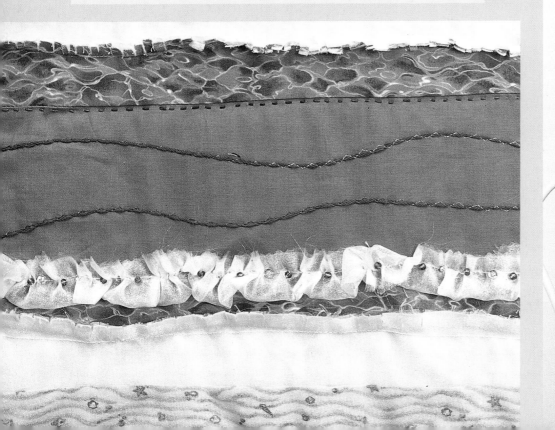

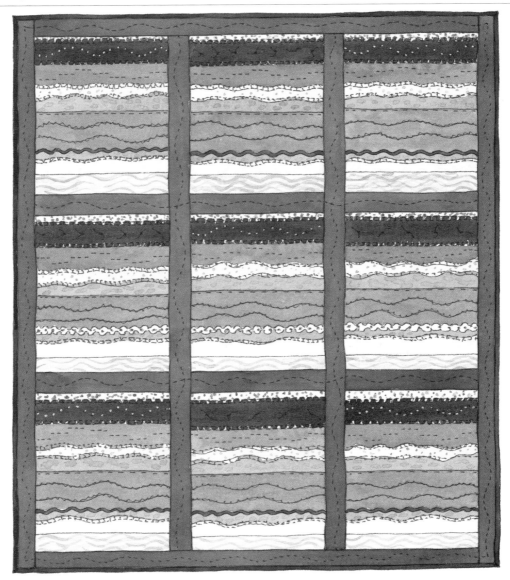

Finished size: 55½ x 47½ in/141 x 120.5 cm

MATERIALS

All fabrics used in the quilt top are 45 in/115 cm wide, 100% cotton apart from the organza, which is 54 in/137 cm wide.

For the blocks:
Plain sky blue: 25 in/64 cm
Dark blue: 7 in/18 cm
Blue denim-style: 7 in/18 cm
Blue/white speckled: 6 in/15 cm
Turquoise water effect: 15 in/38 cm
Cream speckled: 5 in/12.5 cm
Cream swirl: 5 in/12.5 cm
Cream marble: 5 in/12.5 cm
Sand effect print: 7 in/18 cm
Cream twinkle organza: 15 in/38 cm

For the embellishments:
1 skein thick mid-blue coton perlé embroidery thread
White ric-rac braid (or blue if not dyeing):
2¾ yds/2.50 m
Blue cold water dye (optional)
Selection of different blue threads (hand and machine) to match
White twinkle organza: 5 in/12.5 cm
2 packets of small white beads
2 packets of medium silvery-white beads

Sashing and borders: dark air-force blue, 27 in/70 cm, 60 in/150 cm wide
Backing: white-on-blue print, 1½ yds/1.30 m, 60 in/150 cm wide
Batting: 57 x 49 in/145 x 125 cm
Binding: white-on-blue print, 12½ in/32 cm

ALTERNATIVE COLOR SCHEMES

1 A monochrome color scheme in grey, black and white is very dramatic, using colors not normally used in a patchwork; 2 Using printed fabrics here hints of grasses, bushes and sand; 3 Purples, pinks and some fun fabrics make a vibrant scheme that would be perfect for a young girl; 4 The hand-dyed fabrics used here work well together.

1

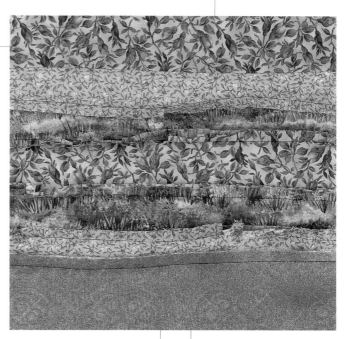

2

3

4

CUTTING

1 From the plain sky blue fabric, cut six strips, 4 in/10 cm deep, across the width of the fabric.

2 From the dark blue fabric, cut three strips, 2¼ in/6 cm deep, across the width of the fabric.

3 From the blue denim-style fabric, cut three strips, 2¼ in/6 cm deep, across the width of the fabric.

4 From the blue/white speckled fabric, cut three strips, 2 in/5 cm deep, across the width of the fabric.

5 From the turquoise water effect fabric, cut three strips, 5 in/12.5 cm deep, across the width of the fabric.

6 The cream speckled, cream swirl and cream marble fabrics are already the correct size (5 in/12.5 cm).

7 From the sand effect print, cut three strips, 2¼ in/6 cm deep, across the width of the fabric.

8 From the cream twinkle organza, cut three strips, 5 in/12.5 cm deep, across the width of the fabric.

9 From the dark air-force blue fabric, cut two strips, 2 in/5.5 cm deep, across the width of the fabric for the short horizontal sashing. Cross-cut these into six 13½ in/34.5 cm lengths. Cut two strips, 2½ in/6.5 cm deep, for the long vertical sashing and trim to 51½ in/131 cm.

10 From the dark air-force blue fabric, also cut four strips, 2½ in/6.5 cm deep, across the width of the fabric for the borders.

11 From the white-on-blue print fabric, cut five strips, 2 in/5 cm deep, across the width of the fabric for the binding.

STITCHING THE STRIP SETS

The blocks in the quilt are created from different strips of fabric, joined in different ways (see quilt plan). First, the long strips cut across the width of the fabric are joined, then these are cross-cut to form the individual blocks.

1 With right sides uppermost, lay a strip of dark blue fabric on top of a strip of denim-style fabric. Then take a strip of blue speckled fabric and place it together with the double-thickness dark blue/denim strip so that the wrong side of the denim is facing the wrong side of the speckled fabric. Taking a ¼ in/0.75 cm seam allowance, stitch along one long edge so that the seam allowance is on the right side of the work (i.e. opposite to normal). Repeat twice more and put these three strip sets aside for later.

NOTE When the block in step 1 is assembled, the denim fabric will be hidden under the dark blue fabric. It will show only at the frayed seam allowances, which are visible on the right side of the work.

2 Take one cream strip and one turquoise strip and lay them one on top of the other on your cutting board, right sides up. Starting from one short end and cutting away from you, use your rotary cutter to cut a slightly wavy line along the center of the strip (diagram 1). Separate the two halves, then take the top cream strip and put it together with the bottom turquoise strip. Similarly, take the top turquoise strip and put it together with the bottom cream strip. Keep these two pairs of different fabrics together.

diagram 1

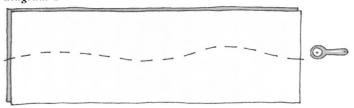

3 Repeat step 2 twice more, pairing each of the remaining two cream strips with a turquoise strip, then cutting and pairing up as described (six pairs in total).

4 With wrong sides facing, pin together the pairs of cream and turquoise strips along their wavy edges (diagram 2a). Taking a ¼ in/0.75 cm seam allowance, stitch the curved seams, easing them gently together. Make sure that the seam allowances show on the right side of the work, i.e. opposite to normal (diagram 2b). Repeat to make six strips of two-tone fabric in all.

diagram 2a

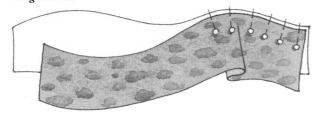

diagram 2b

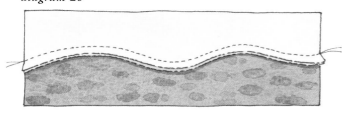

5 Take one of the cream/turquoise strips and, with right sides together, stitch a strip of the sand effect print to the cream strip, using a normal straight seam. The sand effect print will form the bottom of the blocks. Repeat with two more of the cream/turquoise strips and sand effect strips.

6 Lay one of the remaining cream/turquoise strips on your cutting board. Lay the edge of a sky blue strip over the cream strip, so that it overlaps the cream strip by about 2 in/5 cm. Cut a slightly wavy line centrally along the length of the overlap (diagram 3) and discard the underneath fabric. Pin and stitch the sky

diagram 3

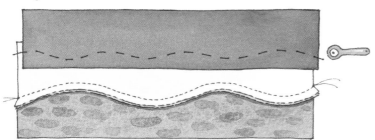

blue strip to the cream strip along the wavy edge as in step 4 (i.e. with seam allowances showing on the right side). Trim the unsewn edge of the sky blue strip so that the strip measures about 2¾ in/7 cm deep. Repeat with the remaining two cream/turquoise strips.

7 Take one of the dark blue/denim/speckled strip sets made in step 1, and one of the cream/turquoise/sky blue strip sets made in step 6. With the wrong side of the denim strip facing the wrong side of the sky blue strip, pin and stitch together along the long edge (i.e. with seam allowances showing on the right side).

8 Take one of the cream/turquoise/sand effect strip sets you made in step 5. With right sides together and a normal straight seam, stitch a 4 in/10 cm sky blue strip to the turquoise strip. Repeat twice more. Then stitch the sky blue strip to the turquoise strip of the strip set made in step 7.

9 Finally, take a cream organza strip and lay it over the bottom two strips (sand effect and cream). Pin in place and topstitch with matching thread, leaving a raggy edge.

10 Repeat steps 7–9 twice more. This completes the three strip sets required for the quilt. Double-check the order of fabrics in each strip set, starting from the top. It should be as follows: blue speckled fabric; dark blue/denim double layer; sky blue; cream; turquoise; sky blue; turquoise; cream; sand effect. Check the depth of your strip sets – from top to bottom, they should measure 16½ in/42 cm. Trim them down if necessary.

ADDING SOME EMBELLISHMENTS

Now your basic strips are complete, you can begin the embellishments. Some embellishments are put on before quilting, some after quilting.

1   For the raggy edges, use small, sharp scissors to snip into the seam allowances that show on the right side of the work, making your cuts about ¼ in/ 0.75 cm apart. Refer to diagram 4 for the placement of the raggy edges.

diagram 4

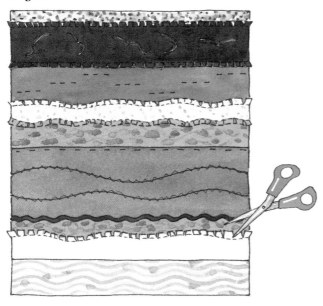

NOTE   The raggy edges will improve in appearance the more you handle the quilt, so cut these before adding the other embellishments.

2   For the couching on each strip set, cut two lengths of mid-blue cotton perlé thread at least 4 in/ 10 cm longer than the strip set. Set your machine to a zigzag stitch, lay the first thread down along the wide sky blue strip and stitch over the top, adjusting the position of the thread as you go to achieve a wavy effect. Repeat with the second thread. Trim off the thread ends. Repeat for the remaining two strip sets.

3   If you want to dye your ric-rac, use a blue cold water dye and follow the instructions on page 24. Using a matching thread, stitch the ric-rac above the lower turquoise strips on two of the strip sets. (The third strip set will be embellished with gathered strips of organza after the quilting is complete.)

ADDING THE SASHING AND BORDERS

1   Press the three strip sets from the back, avoiding ironing the cream organza.

2   Now cross-cut the three strip sets into nine blocks 13½ in/34.5 cm wide. Lay the blocks out on the floor in rows of three and adjust their positions until you are happy with the arrangement. In the quilt in the photograph on page 97, the three blocks across the center are the ones without ric-rac.

3   Using a ¼ in/0.75 cm seam allowance, pin and stitch the short horizontal dark air-force blue sashing strips in between the blocks to make three columns of three blocks. Press the seam allowances towards the sashing. Then pin and stitch the two long vertical sashing strips in between the three columns. Press the seam allowances towards the sashing.

NOTE   Don't worry if the layers, or strata, within each block do not line up completely with those in a neighboring block. Due to the nature of the strippy patchwork and the curved piecing, the layers will not be perfectly aligned.

4   Measure the pieced top through the center from side to side, then trim two dark air-force blue border strips to this measurement. Taking the usual seam allowance, pin and stitch the border strips to the top and bottom of the quilt. Press the seam allowances towards the borders.

5   Finally, measure the pieced top through the center from top to bottom, then trim the two remaining border strips to this measurement. Taking the usual seam allowance, pin and stitch the border strips to the sides of the quilt, taking care to line up the blocks. Press the seam allowances towards the borders.

FINISHING

1 Remove the selvages from the backing and spread, right side down, on a flat surface, then smooth out the batting and the pieced top, right side up, on top. Fasten together with safety pins or baste in a grid.

2 Using a walking foot, quilt in-the-ditch (see page 9) around all the main blocks to stabilize them.

3 Using dark blue thread, quilt wavy lines along all the sashing and border strips.

4 Using a matching cotton perlé thread, quilt the sky blue areas with big hand stitches, following the quilt plan.

5 Cut the 5 in/12.5 cm strip of white twinkle organza crossways into three. Fold the strips in half lengthways, then trim back the raw edges, so that the folded strip measures 1 in/2.5 cm. You may wish to

do this with pinking shears to prevent fraying. Run a long gathering thread centrally along the strips and pull up the thread to gather. Stitch above the lower turquoise strips on the blocks that do not have ric-rac braid stitched to them. Add further embellishment by stitching medium-sized beads along the organza.

6 Add small white beads to some of the dark blue strips (see page 18) as shown on the quilt plan.

7 In the other dark blue strips, add a few tie quilting stitches made with cotton perlé thread (see page 25).

8 When all the embellishments are complete, trim off any excess batting and backing so they are even with the quilt top. Join the binding strips with diagonal seams to make a continuous length to fit all around the quilt and use to bind the edges with a double-fold binding, mitered at the corners (see page 11).

Square Dance

Designed by Eilean MacDonald

This interesting wallhanging combines symmetry and movement, symbolizing the energy of a square dance. The quilting is done by hand using thick embroidery cotton and varies from closely worked stitches to widely spaced ones, creating a three-dimensional effect on the surface of the hanging. By dyeing your own fabric, you can give the quilt a unique touch. You could also experiment with using different colors of threads in different sections – the permutations are endless.

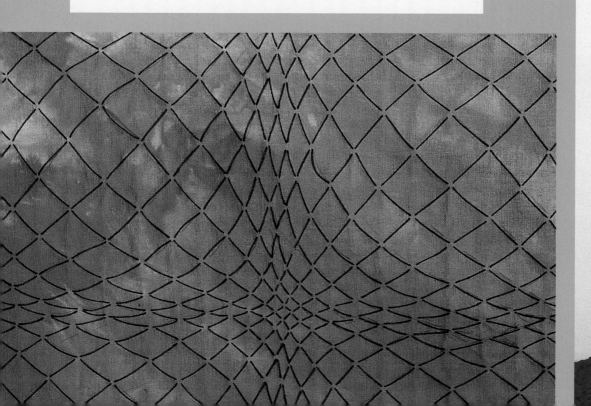

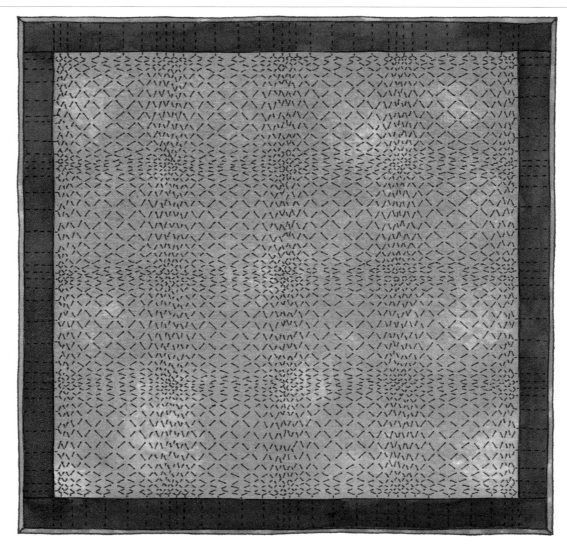

Finished size: 44 x 44 in/111.5 x 111.5 cm

MATERIALS

All fabrics used in the quilt top are 100% cotton and 56 in/143 cm wide.

If dyeing your own fabric:

Total amount of white fabric required: 3½ yds/3.40 m

Dyes: one box each of light blue, mid-blue and navy blue. I used a hot water dye, but if your fabric is 100% cotton a cold water dye would also work. Do not use a machine dye. If you wish, you can mix powder dyes to create your own color tones. Just make samples and keep copious notes on the colors and quantities of dyes and fabrics used. Keep samples of your dyeing results for future reference.

If buying pre-colored fabric:

Quilt top (including binding): mid-blue, 1½ yds/ 1.40 m

Borders: dark blue, 18 in/56 cm

Backing and hanging sleeve: light blue, 1½ yds/ 1.40 m, 56 in/143 cm wide

Batting: high loft, 1½ yds/1.40 m, 56 in/143 cm wide

You will also need:

Sheet of letter paper, 8½ x 11 in

Sheet of tracing paper, 11 x 17 in

Matching machine thread

Coton Perlé No.5: four balls navy blue; one ball light blue

Crewel needle

ALTERNATIVE COLOR SCHEMES

1 The use of pale dyed fabric with darker stitching creates a pretty pink variation for a little girl's room; 2 The apricot fabric and variegated thread gives a fun alternative that would appeal to any child; 3 Using two strong colors together, a purple ground and a contrast green thread with subtle tonal variation produces a striking, modern effect; 4 Using a reversed color scheme again, a black fabric stitched with a shimmering green thread produces a stunning and dramatic effect.

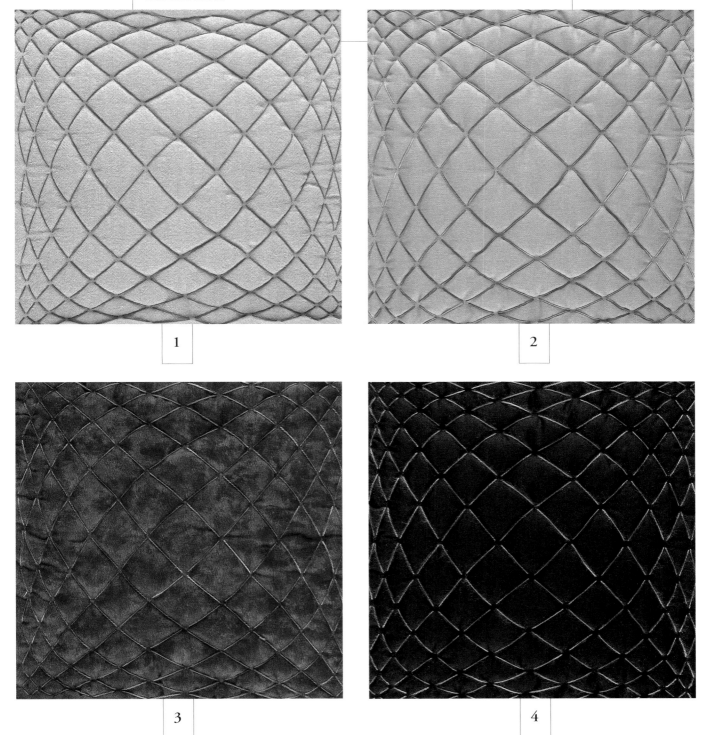

1

2

3

4

CUTTING AND DYEING

1 If you are dyeing the colors yourself, cut the white fabric into three pieces across the width as follows:

1½ yds/1.4 m for the top and binding (to be dyed mid-blue)

18 in/56 cm for the borders (to be dyed navy blue)

1½ yds/1.4 m for the backing and hanging sleeve (to be dyed light blue).

2 Wash the fabric before dyeing to remove any finishing or treatments.

3 Make up the mid-blue dye bath following the manufacturer's instructions. Re-wet the fabric for the top and binding if necessary and wring out excess water. Loosen the fabric and immerse it in the dye bath. To create the subtle mottled effect, DO NOT STIR OR AGITATE THE FABRIC. Leave for the given time. When the dyeing time is over, set the dye following the manufacturer's instructions.

4 Repeat the dyeing process twice more with the remaining pieces of fabric, using the navy blue and light blue dyes.

CREATING THE DESIGN

1 Using a pencil, draw a square grid of graduated size onto the sheet of letter paper, with the lines ³⁄₁₆ in/ 5 mm, ¼ in/7 mm, ³⁄₈ in/1 cm, ½ in/13 mm, ⅝ in/ 16 mm, ¾ in/2 cm, ³⁄₁₆ in/21 mm and 1 in/26 mm apart (diagram 1). The finished square should measure 4½ x 4½ in/11.8 x 11.8 cm.

diagram 1

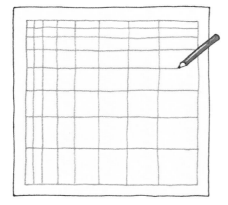

2 Place a sheet of tracing paper over the grid and create a second grid by drawing diagonally across the squares and rectangles formed by the first grid (diagram 2).

diagram 2

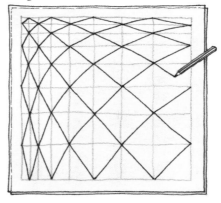

3 Remove the original grid and you are left with a tracing as in diagram 3. This forms a quarter of one block.

diagram 3

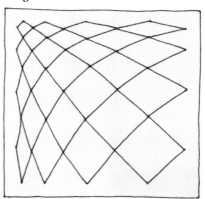

4 Working on the 11 x 17 in sheet of tracing paper, trace the second grid three times as mirror images to create a larger square block (diagram 4). Alternatively, if you prefer to use a computer, scan the grid and print out four quarter blocks which you can then stick together with tape.

diagram 4

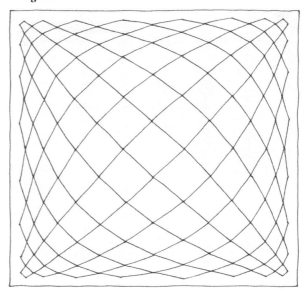

5 The complete design is created by repeating the block in four rows of four. By varying the column widths of the original grid you can produce very different effects, so when you feel confident, experiment and create your own design. (So that the design will repeat, remember always to use an even number of columns.)

CUTTING

1 From the mid-blue fabric, cut a square, 38½ x 38½ in/98 x 98 cm, for the quilt top.

2 From the mid-blue fabric, cut four strips, 2½ in/6 cm deep, across the width of the fabric, for the binding.

3 From the navy blue fabric, cut two strips, 4 x 38½ in/10 x 98 cm, and two strips, 4 x 46½ in/ 10 x 119 cm, for the borders.

4 From the light blue fabric, cut a square, 46½ x 46½ in/119 x 119 cm, for the backing.

5 From the light blue fabric, cut a strip, 7 x 41 in/ 18 x 104 cm, for the hanging sleeve.

MAKING THE WALLHANGING

1 Mark the center of the mid-blue fabric square and, using dressmaker's carbon paper, transfer the four center blocks onto the fabric. Then, working outwards, transfer the other blocks. Alternatively, use a light box to transfer the blocks.

NOTE If you don't have a light box, a good method of transferring the design is to stick it to a window with the fabric on top and trace the lines through. Then move the fabric along to the position for the next block.

2 Taking a ¼ in/0.75 cm seam allowance, pin and stitch the two 4 x 38½ in/10 x 98 cm navy blue border strips to opposite sides of the mid-blue square. Press the seam allowances towards the borders.

3 Taking the usual seam allowance, pin and stitch the two 4 x 46½ in/10 x 119 cm navy blue border strips to the top and bottom. Trim the ends of the strips to level the edges.

QUILTING THE WALLHANGING

1 Remove the selvages from the backing and spread, right side down, on a flat surface, then smooth out the batting and the pieced top, right side up, on top. Fasten together with safety pins or baste in a grid.

2 Using the navy blue coton perlé and a crewel needle, stitch the grid design through all three layers, starting in the center and working out towards the edges. Use one stitch per line and allow approximately ⅛ in/3 mm between stitches (diagram 5).

diagram 5

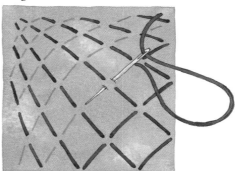

NOTE Where the stitches are large, a high loft will be created; where they are smaller, a flatter effect will be obtained.

3 When the central design is complete, trim the edges so that the borders measure 3 in/8 cm in width. Use a quilting marker to draw a straight line from each end point of the design across the width of the border. Using the light blue coton perlé, quilt the lines with stitches approximately ⅜ in/8 mm long.

FINISHING

1 Join the binding strips with diagonal seams to make a continuous length to fit all around the quilt and use to bind the edges with a double-fold binding, mitered at the corners (see page 11).

2 Take the 7 x 41 in/18 x 104 cm strip for the hanging sleeve and fold in half lengthways with right sides together. Using a ¼ in/6 mm seam allowance, stitch along the long edge to form a tube. Press the seam flat along the center of the tube. Stitch across one short end. Turn right side out, press with the seam along the center back, turn in the other short end and slipstitch. Slipstitch to the back of the hanging.

110 THE CONTRIBUTORS

Jane Coombes is a qualified patchwork and quilting tutor who gives workshops and lectures.

Sarah Fincken works as a textile artist, teaching patchwork and quilting. She also designs, exhibits and writes.

Nikki Foley has a certificate in interior design and uses this to her advantage when designing quilts and patterns for her business, The Sewing Shed (www.thesewingshed@aol.com).

Janet Goddard writes patterns for magazines and books and teaches quilting also.

Eilean MacDonald studied for a B.A. in Contemporary Textile Practice and now undertakes private commissions for her textured textile creations.

Gail Smith opened her shop, Abigail Crafts, after completing a City and Guild course; she is a qualified adult education teacher, running local quilting groups.

Sarah Wellfair is a qualified teacher who runs a full program of workshops from her quilt shop, Goose Chase Quilting.

Sheilah Daughtree holds an Arts Degree and specializes in quilting, regularly contributing articles to *Patchwork and Quilting* magazine.

ACKNOWLEDGMENTS

The publishers would like to thank the following companies for kindly supplying the silk ribbons used in the "Flying Geese and Roses" quilt:

CK Media, 57 Kiln Ride, Wokingham, Berkshire RG40 3PJ
Email: media@thekingdoms.co.uk

Ribbon Designs, PO Box 382, Edgware, Middlesex HA8 7XQ
Email: tradesales@silkribbon.co.uk

INDEX